LAOS CAMBODIA

TRAVEL GUIDE

INCLUDES FREE BOOK: MUAY THAI TRAINING

WHY YOU NEED TO TRAIN IN THAILAND

TABLE OF CONTENTS

- TABLE OF CONTENTS 2
- LAOS TRAVEL GUIDE 5
- INTRODUCTION 6
- AN INTRODUCTION TO LAOS 8
- Getting Into Laos 14
- CURRENCY AND LANGUAGE 18
- EATING AND SHOPPING 22
- Things to Do and See in Laos 28
- CONCLUSION 42
- CAMBODIA TRAVEL GUIDE 43
- INTRODUCTION 44
- The History of Cambodia 46
    - HISTORY 47
- GETTING INTO CAMBODIA 51
    - VISAS 51
    - OVERSTAYING IN CAMBODIA 53
- Getting Around in Cambodia 55
- The Language of Cambodia 58
- Staying Safe in Cambodia 61
    - CRIME 61
    - STAYING HEALTHY 62

MAKING PURCHASES IN CAMBODIA	65
EATING	72
DRINKS	73
THINGS TO SEE IN CAMBODIA	77
CONCLUSION	96
WHY YOU NEED	97
TO	97
TRAIN IN THAILAND	97
INTRODUCTION	99
STRESS FREE LIFE SAY BYE TO THE BULLSHIT	101
LIKEMINDED PEOPLE	104
MUAY THAI SPORTS CAPITAL	108
MMA GROWING FAST	111
BEAUTIFUL WEATHER AND SCENERY	113
LEVERAGING YOUR MONEY	114
COST OF LIVING	115
HOUSING CHOICES	117
CITIES TO LIVE IN	119
BANGKOK	119
PHUKET	119
CHIANG MAI	120
PATTAYA	123
THAILAND FOOD	124
FREE TIME ACTIVITIES	124
CHEAP SHOPPING	125

MASSAGES FOR ABOUT FIVE DOLLARS	125
BEACHES AND BEAUTIFUL VIEWS	126

PEOPLE FROM ALL AROUND THE WORLD 126
DON'T BRING SAND TO THE BEACH 131

THAI GIRLS	132
FOREIGN GIRLS	134

HOW TO GET TO THAILAND 135

PASSPORT AND VISA	137
CHEAP TICKET	138

GYM SPONSORSHIP 138
HOW TO MAKE MONEY IN THAILAND 141

FIGHTING MUAY THAI	143
BOXING	144
FIGHTING K1	146
FIGHTING MMA	148
OTHER WAYS TO HUSTLE CASH	151
TEACHING ENGLISH	151
ACTING OR MODELING	152
DIGITAL NOMADS	154
OPEN YOUR OWN BUSINESS	154

DON'T BE A PUSSY! TAKE SOME ACTION! 156

LAOS TRAVEL GUIDE

INTRODUCTION

Planning a big vacation can be a huge deal. There are a lot of great things to get in order, and you want to make sure that you are getting all the fun out of the trip that you possibly can. When you are ready to plan out your next big trip, make sure that Laos is on the radar.

Laos is a beautiful country that has so much to offer a tourist. While it may not be the biggest country or the one with the most beaches, you will be surprised by how many different things there are for you to do while in the country. From all the great hiking paths to kayaking, visiting temples, relaxing, and even seeing some of the local freshwater dolphins that have helped explorers for years, you are sure to find something for everyone who is traveling with you.

Planning out a trip to Laos takes some time and preparation. You want to make sure to pick the best activities while also staying within your budget. There are also time constraints, tickets to purchase, and making sure that everyone has the right visas to get into the country without causing trouble. Figuring all this out on your own can sometimes seem impossible.

That is where this guidebook is going to come into play. This guidebook is full of all the information that you need to ensure you are ready to have the best time possible on your trip to Laos. Whether you want to have the biggest adventure or just spend time getting to know the local people and have fun, there is sure to be something for everyone.

When you are ready to get started on planning that great Laos vacation, make sure to pick up this book and find out everything that you will need.

AN INTRODUCTION TO LAOS

Laos is a small country that is often forgotten in Southeast Asia. While other countries like Vietnam and Cambodia are busy promoting themselves so much, many forget that Laos is a great place for you to come and visit. But taking the time to come and see this country is definitely worth it, especially if you're looking for a culture that is laid back and doesn't mind watching a beautiful sunset on the Mekong River.

If you are on a tight budget, you should be aware that this place is a bit more expensive compared to some of the neighboring countries like Thailand. But the prices are still pretty affordable for the area and you are going to have the best of times when you can get out and meet some of the locals. Plan some of the trip ahead of time, and you will be doing late.

So let's look at some of the history that comes with this country. Laos is a small country that is squeezed in between some bigger countries. It was first made into an entity by the warlord Fa Ngum in 1353. This warlord declared himself as the king of Lane Xang. This was originally a vassal state of the Khmer, but there was a succession dispute and in 1694, this kingdom was split into three different parts. The Siamese soon started to devour this area piece by piece and then in 1885, the remaining parts agreed to work with the Siamese for protection.

At about this time, the French began moving into the area and they wanted to get some of this area back. The French were successful in getting some of the area east of the Mekong back and they used this as kind of a buffer to

Vietnam. Laos became a unified territory in 1907. This area was then occupied by the Japanese in 1945, and for the next 30 years the French and the Japanese fought for control of this area. Finally, it received its full independence in 1953, but the war continued between various factions including the Pathet Lao, the French monarchy, and the Communist party.

After the fall of Saigon in 1975, and many years of bombing by the United States, the Pathet Lao, a Communist party, took control of the area of Vientiane and was able to end the monarchy in that area. While this initially started out as closer ties to socialization and Vietnam, the culture in that area slowly turned to foreign investments and more private enterprises until they were eventually admitted to the ASEAN in 1997.

While this country is just an hour from Bangkok, the people of this area are still living life the way they have done for hundreds of years, although this is starting to slowly change. Since this country is nestled between some bigger ones and often forgotten, tourism is not a big thing in the area, but the government is trying to turn this around. In the past, the amount of monks in Laos far outnumbered the amount of tourists in the area, but it looks like that trend is starting to change for this country.

If you are looking to visit an area that has a wide diversity of cultures, look no further than Laos. This area doesn't have very many people, but you will be able to see a combination of 49 different tribes and ethnic groups, although Hmong, Khmou, and Lao are the biggest three. Most of the tribes are pretty small, many of which just have a few hundred people all together. Laos is officially a Buddhist country and since the fall of communism, the national symbol has gone from the hammer and sickle to the gilded stupa of the Pha That Luang. Despite this change, there are still some remnants of Communism in the country so be aware of that.

According to the customs of Lao, women in the area must wear a long sarong in their regional patterns, known as a phaa sin. Of course, many of the minorities in the country have some of their own styles of clothing and you can often find some Vietnamese influences, including the conical hat from that area. It is becoming more common for the people to wear clothes that are more similar to the clothes found in the Western world and the traditional clothes are saved for special holidays and festivals. The traditional clothing is still required for ceremonies and when present in government offices.

There are three seasons that are present in Laos and you should take these into consideration when planning your trip and figuring out what activities to do. These seasons include:

- March to May—this is the hot season. You will find that the temperatures often get above 100 degrees. Tourism is not big in this time because the country is landlocked and it is hard to find ways to cool down.
- May to October—the temperatures are a bit better in this time, coming in at about 30 degrees Celsius. It is not uncommon during this time to have lots of tropical downpours, especially in July and August, which is why the season is called the wet season. In some y ears, the Mekong River will flood over so be really careful if you go out during this time.
- November to March—this is known as the dry season. The temperatures can get as low as 15 degrees Celsius, although it is possible to be warmer and the amount of rainfall is low. This is the time when most tourists are going to show up, so be aware of this. Be aware that during the end of this season, many of the northern areas, anything north of Luang Prabang, will have some issues with haze because of fires and farmers burning their fields.

It is up to your discretion on when to head out to Laos. While November to March are often the best times to go in terms of weather, this is also when all the other tourists are going and you will have to fight with all other people. Going during the other times of the year can bring out some problems, so do some research and see which ones are the best for you so you can have a great trip.

When you are in Laos, make sure to be respectful. Don't go and look like you are heading to the beach all of the time. Instead, wear appropriate attire because this area is still very traditional. In addition, if you ever head to one of the temples, remember that this is a place of worship and you will quickly get in a lot of trouble if you don't behave. When you enter temples and private homes, always take off your shoes to show respect. Other things to keep in mind is to never show the soles of your feet, don't touch someone else's head, and never be drunk out in public, even though drinking is allowed.

Things in the country of Laos go at their own speed. Often, things are not going to happen at the exact time that you schedule them. While this can be really frustrating for many foreigners, you must make sure that you stay calm because anger is looked down upon in this country. Keep extra respect for the monks of the area; some take vows of silence and will not be able to talk to you and taking photos with them is usually frowned upon.

Be careful about being safe when you're in Laos. You should always carry around your passport and visa to show any time someone asks. If you are not able to produce this information, you will have to pay a fine. The crime levels are pretty low in this country, although in high tourist areas you should make sure that you are watching your belongings carefully as petty theft can happen. Don't use drugs when you are in the country. This is a huge problem in Laos and the law doesn't really make a distinction between trafficking drugs or using it for yourself. If caught, the law really isn't going to be on your side and you will get expulsion and high fines if you're lucky, but more likely imprisonment. Just stay away from drugs and anything else illegal and you will have a much better time.

In regards to your health, make sure that you are up to date on your vaccines before leaving. Malaria is common in quite a bit of Laos as well as other diseases spread by bugs so bring insect repellent along. Bottled water is best in this area so stick with this. There are several medical clinics, especially in the area of Vientiane that are associated with European embassies so you can get some good treatment there. If you aren't in the area, it is possible to go to Thailand for treatment of serious illnesses. It is best to just be careful just in case you are in an area that doesn't have good medical treatment and always carry travel medical insurance when you are out of the country to ensure you are getting proper care.

Traveling to Laos is a great experience, you just need to know some of the customs as well as how you should behave. Once you get this part down, it is much easier to find your way around and you will have the best time possible.

Getting Into Laos

Now let's take some time to go through and find out what all is needed in order to get into Laos. You are not allowed to just walk right into the country, even though the government has been looking to increase the number of tourists that come into the country. Without the right kind of paperwork, you will not be allowed into the country or could face high penalties. No matter which part of the world you are coming from, it is best to get your paperwork all in place ahead of time. It is possible to do it upon arrival, but who would want to start their vacation doing all this work and hoping it goes through when they could get it done ahead of time and start exploring right away?

Visas

If you are from Switzerland, Japan, Korea, or Russia as well as any of the ASEAN countries, you do not need a visa in order to get into Laos. Al other tourists will need a tourist visa if staying for under two months and it needs to be issued by the Lao consulate or embassy. It is possible to get a visa when you arrive in one of the airports, but this can sometimes take a bit of time and most people like to just make sure the paperwork is all done upfront. Prices for your visa are pretty standard, ranging between $30 to $42 depending on where you are getting the visa from. In most cases, the visa can be done in just a few days. There are some instances when you will be able to get the visa in just a few hours, but be aware that these can get delayed and often cost quite a bit more so it probably isn't the best idea to do this.

If you purchase your visa and other information ahead of time, make sure to carry it with you when you get into the country. While it is possible to get into Laos by land or on an airplane, you will still need to present the proper paperwork to avoid issues later on. Have some photo identification present as well in order to avoid delays when you get off your plane.

Be careful with purchasing visas when you get to the country. These are often more expensive since you need the paperwork before leaving the building than they would be ordering online. While most officials will give you the right price, some may try to charge you extra for the visa and it is difficult to just leave and get one someplace else. In addition, make sure to update your visa or talk to the right authorities if the visa is about to expire and you need to stay for longer. It is much easier to get your extensions ahead of time rather than trying to talk your way out of trouble once you're caught.

Traveling Around Laos

There are many ways that you can travel around the country of Laos and the one that you choose is often going to vary depending on how far you need to go and how fast you are needing to get to the location. Some of the ways that you can get around Laos include:

- Plane—Lao Airlines is pretty much the online airline inside of Laos that you can use. They had a bad history in the past, but thanks to some government regulations, they have gotten much better. Their flights go all over the country and make long trips take just minutes to finish. If you need to go to a remote location, Xian MA60 is the best option, but many of these flights can be cancelled without warning so don't rely on them too much.

- Road—many of the highways in Laos are really nice, but many of them are still unpaved. If you are going between some of the major cities in the country, you will notice they are paved, but anywhere that is more remote will be more difficult. You can use converted truck, minibus, and bus in order to travel on these roads.
- Songthaew—this is a truck based vehicle that has bench seats towards the back, and one on both sides. This is a common travel means and you can find that this is a nice way to travel all together with your group.
- Tuk-tuk—this is s a common way of moving around in Southeast Asia. They usually have three wheels and then are moved around by a bicyclist or a motorcyclist so you can just sit back and relax. The rates are pretty reasonable and this is a unique way to get through and see all the sights.
- Motorcycle—this is the method that you should use if you're looking for a way to travel all on your own. Use Pakse when in Laos because they allow you to rent out a motorcycle the whole time you are in Laos and you know they are well made and safe. Take these all around the country, on dirt roads and more, without feeling like you have to wait for a tour group.
- Bicycle—while you probably don't want to travel through the whole country traveling on a bike, this is a good way to go see some of your favorite sights. There are a ton of tour groups that will take you all around and this mode of transportation allows you to see the world in a different way.
- Boat—while Laos is a landlocked country, there are still several times when you are able to get on a boat to travel around. Whether you are on a chartered boat or speed boat, or one of the other options, you will be able to enjoy the Mekong River and all the sights around it.

As you can see, there are tons of ways that you can get around the country of Laos. Whether you are interested in trying out something new or want to make sure that you are getting the very most when you travel through this country, you are sure to find the right transportation method for you.

CURRENCY AND LANGUAGE

First, let's look at the language of Laos. The official language of this country is known as Lao. It is closely related to Thai and most of the people in Laos also know quite a bit of Thai so if you know some of this language, you should have a pretty easy time getting around. The locals in Laos do appreciate it when you speak in their language so learning a few phrases can be helpful. In addition, many younger people in the area have learned English in school so this language is becoming more well-known in the area, though most of the time their proficiency is going to be low.

In some areas, you are going to find a lot of people who speak some French, leftover from the days when the French were taking over this area. There are still some signs and understanding of this language by the older generations though, but for the most part, the general trend is towards learning more English. Don't be surprised if some school children ask to practice some English with you as this is sometimes used as part of their curriculum requirements. They may talk to you a bit and then ask you to take a picture or sign a form in order to show that they actually did the conversation. Don't get upset with this; rather, see it as a way for you to get to know the local people a bit more and even to get more ideas on what to see while you are in the country.

There are two ways to turn the script for their language into the Latin alphabet. You can do this in the French style or the English style. In Laos, you will find that most government documents are done in the French style but it is becoming more common to see the English spellings since more people are learning this language.

When you are in Laos, you will be using their local currency of the kip. Since Laos joined the stock market in 2011, it is now possible to exchange this coin in some of the neighboring countries so this makes it easier if you are looking to go to more than one country on your trip. As of 2014, 1 US. Dollar equaled 8,000 kip and one Euro is 10,000 kip so be ready to see very large numbers on the prices that you are going to.

The largest note that you can find in Laos is the 100,000 kip, and it is not very common. Usually the common denominations will be between 500 to 50,000.

Depending on the area that you are visiting, you may be able to use your American money, but it is best to go and find how to change your money over. Many of the rural areas won't have the option to use your American or European money and it is just easier to have the kip rather than trying to find places that accept your personal currency.

You may want to consider exchanging your money before getting to Laos. While you can use the ATM's and your card to get money over there, you will often have to pay a fee for the cash advances on the card as well as a fee to exchange the money. This is going to get pretty expensive in no time and it is much better to just have the money on hand. And if you are outside of one of the major cities in Laos, you will find that it is pretty much impossible to even do this, so bringing plenty of cash along is the best option. If you do need more cash while in the country, go and visit one of the banks. These are the easiest ways to get money, they offer the best rates, and you are sure to get real money (instead of risking getting fake money from somewhere else) so you can go and enjoy your trip.

The costs in Laos are pretty reasonable, although you need to watch out for dishonest shop owners who will try to get as much out of you as possible and aren't the nicest. You will find that the prices in Laos are more expensive compared to Cambodia and Thailand so keep this in mind if you are heading to Laos after being in those countries. The dishes you order will be smaller and the hotels are usually not as high of quality for the amount you are spending.

A good rule of thumb when traveling in Laos is to have about $40 USD to get by. You can find reasonable rates on rooms varying from $6 to $15 a night depending on where you stay. Meals can be done for under $5, even for the most elaborate dishes and riding a slow boat all throughout the country can cost as low as $25. As you can see, unless you spend to go all out with shopping or doing the most expensive tourist trips, you can have a great time on a low budget in this country.

EATING AND SHOPPING

Part of the experience of going to Laos is learning more about the culture. And the best way to learn the culture is through the food, drinks, and shopping experiences that they have to offer. Each country is going to have something different to offer, no matter how similar are to another country. While you are in Laos, make sure to go through some of these traditional meals and drinks and go through some of the options available for shopping to get the most out of your trip to Laos.

Eating

When you are in Laos, you have to try out some of the delicious food that is available. Nothing makes a trip better than trying out food that the locals enjoy and seeing how it varies from what you like to eat. The cuisine in Laos is similar to what you would find in the northern part of Thailand and has a lot of spice, bitter tastes, and the locals like to use fresh herbs and raw vegetables. Often the raw vegetables will help to keep your mouth cool when the spices just become too much.

Rice is one of the staples of this culture and usually they will use what is known as sticky rice, which is eaten with the hands from a small bowl. To eat this kind of rice, you will use the right hand, pinch a bit off, roll into a small ball, dip into your sauce or other side, and then eat it all up.

The national dish of Laos is laap. This is basically a salad that has lots of chili powder, lime juice, spices, herbs, and some kind of minced meat. This version uses raw meat in it, although you can cook up the meat if you would like. Seafood is a great option as well and if you have this prepared for you, you will be surprised at how spicy it can be.

Another god dish is tam maak hung which is a papaya salad that is spicy and uses fermented crab and a fish sauce. This is stronger in flavor compared to the similar Thai version and again has a lot of spice in it. Ping kai, a grilled chicken, and mok pa, fish that is steamed are other options that you should try out when you are in Laos.

If you aren't a big fan of all that spicy food, it is easy to get ahold of some imported food from other cultures and countries that are close to Laos. Khao jii pat-te, a French baguettes and foe noodles from China are really great snacks or breakfast foods that you can pick from. Give a few different things a try and you are sure to find something that you will love that is completely different than you will find back at home.

Drink

When you are in Laos, not only is it important to enjoy some good food, you should also take the time to find some of the tasty local drinks along the way. To start, the legal drinking age is 18 in Laos. But you have to drink the alcoholic beverage on the property you bought it, such as at the bar or a restaurant. There is no legal drinking age when you leave the premises where you drink. This also means you should not get completely drunk when you are at these establishments. Laos doesn't have any tolerance for drunk driving and if you're caught, you could spend quite a bit of time in prison.

The official drink in Laos is Beer Lao, a drink that is made using Laotian jasmine rice and is actually one of the only things that Laos exports. You can choose between light, dark, and original and it is fairly inexpensive to get. This is a tasty option that people all over the world love and you can easily add into your favorites.

Lao-lao is a rice spirit that you can try and is a really cheap way to get drunk in no time. In fact, one bottle can cost you just $0.30. Be careful about drinking this though since the distilling standards and the quality will vary between who makes it and you will likely never get the same kind again.

Unless you are in Vang Vieng or Vientiane, you are not going to find all that much for nightlife in the country. This means that if you want to have a drink at the end of the night, you will just go to a regular restaurant.

Lao coffee is really high quality and is sure to get you ready for seeing more sights while you are going through the country. The beans are grown in the south at Bolaven Plateau. Unlike coffees that you find in Thailand, the Lao coffee does not use tamarind seed to add flavoring. As a tourist, make sure to ask for kaafeh thung, this ensures that you get the highest quality coffee and not something that is overpriced version that is basically just Nescafe. In most establishments, kaafeh dam is black coffee, kaafew lao is the come with condensed milk and sugar, and kaafeh nom is coffee with milk.

It is usually not a good idea to drink tap water when you are in Laos. It often is not all that clean and could make you feel sick. Luckily, bottled water is really easy to get and won't cost a lot so you will be able to get ahold of plenty of liquid while on your vacation.

These are just a few of the different drinks that are available in Laos for you to try out. If you see something that looks interesting, make sure to ask one of the locals to help you pick. They are more than happy to help and are sure to help you pick out the one that is their favorite.

Shopping

Take some time to go shopping while you are in Laos. There are a ton of great stores, markets, and other places where you can get one of a kind options when it comes to things to show off back home or to give to friends and family. Compared to shopping back at home, you will be able to find items for very inexpensive, so you will be able to make some great purchases without going through your budget too quickly. For example, it is possible to get handmade dresses in some of the biggest cities for just $2-3 per outfit.

Some of the places that you can check out when you are in Laos include:

- Outdoor markets—outdoor markets are prevalent around Laos and offer you an opportunity to look around the village or town while making some purchases as well. These are good places to get some interesting items, food, and even to bargain a bit so you are able to get the best deal possible. Most of the places you will visit will have some variation on this, although some of the best ones will be in the big cities, so take some time to shop and see what is being offered.
- Weaving schools and locations—in some of the villages that are scattered throughout Laos, there are various weaving schools available. These were often started when foreigners came into Laos and wanted to help make sure that the traditional art of weaving was not lost. These schools invite the locals to come and take full classes in this art. In order to keep open though, these locations will offer many

of their wears for sale. Think of all the cool things you will be able to find at these places that are all originals. You can get the items for a good place, or even take a class, and help out one of the local communities in Laos.
- Village stores—Laos is a country full of little villages and many traditional tribes are still around. Many of the tours that you will pick from will allow you to go and see some of these villages and you will be amazed at how much neat stuff you can find in these areas. In addition, the village stores are often just trying to make enough to get by, rather than trying to make a huge profit like the stores in America, so you can get some really amazing deals while getting something that is really unique. If your travels take you to one of these villages, at least go in and find out what all is available and get to know the people of the area much better.
- High end stores—even in Laos you will be able to find some really nice high end stores. Be ready to spend more, but if you want to get really nice items that are unique to Laos and you can't get anywhere else, these are the places you should go to. These are found in high district areas of some of the big towns you will visit and even just going into the store to simply look around can be an experience even if you don't spend any money.

Even if you're not really into shopping, this can be a new and exciting experience when you are in a different country. Laos offers some new options that you just won't be able to find back at home and you can find some great original items that will impress everyone back home. Try out a few of these shopping centers and you are sure to find something that you are going to fall in love with.

Things to Do and See in Laos

Laos is a beautiful country with plenty for you and your family to do. Whether you enjoy being out in the open or want to see some of the history that is found all throughout this country, you will find something for everyone to enjoy. Make sure to visit some of the biggest attractions so you can impress your friends when you get back home, but don't forget about some of those hidden treasures off the beaten path that most tourists don't know about so you can get the true experience while in Laos. When you are ready to get started, check out these great things to do and see while you are in the wonderful country of Laos.

The Gibbon Experience

This location is near Bokeo and it is something that all tourists should take some time to see. It is about three hours out of Huay Xia and then you will need to walk through some of the forest in order to get the infrastructure, so make sure to bring along some of your good shoes so you can make it through. This area is all made up of tree houses that are perched nicely on top of trees more than 40 meters in the air. Think of how up you would have to climb just to get to your home! In order to get to the homes, you will need to glide on some zip lines, something you will be doing until you leave this area.

In order to get into this area, you will have to sign up for a trip and you will be in the Bokeo Nature Reserve for about three days. The number of participants allowed on each trip is limited so make sure that you schedule this with plenty of time to spare so you can get your whole group in. You will love the long trek through the forest, seeing everything from houses that are over 40 meters in the air, and zipping through the trees without a care in the world. Make sure to leave a little donation for the headman of the village; this donation is used to help support the school in this area.

Tour Around Huay Xia

While this is a main attraction in the area, it is a small village and you will be able to take in much of the sights with just one day in the area. The town is situated on a hill that is close to the ferry pier so it is pretty easy to get to and there are quite a few tourist attractions that you can enjoy. First, get up to the little village and take a look at your surroundings. Then head up to the Jom Khao Manilat temple to see the beautiful little village as well as the Mekong River below. You can rent a bicycle and tour the city or go on foot. There are lots of paths to go on, some of the best Laos food around, and so much more to enjoy in this tiny little fishing village.

See a bit of China

Laos is right up next to China and you can visit several spots that allow you to see this wonderful country without ever having to leave Laos or do the extra paperwork. If you head to Luang Namtha, a little town that is about six hours from Huay Xia, you will be able to see all the sights that you would like. There are river plains that you can spend some time relaxing near, or even boating, high mountains that you can hike through, or just take some time to walk through the peaceful and small town on its own. The Chinese boarder is also within reach of this tiny town so you can see even more of the world just from this one small area. You can choose to just spend part of the day in the area, or night camp trips are a popular option to take in more of the scenery.

Dolphin Viewing

If you are in the area of Champasak, make sure to go out to the river and see some Dolphin viewing. While there are many places in the world that allow you to view dolphins, you aren't going to find anywhere else that has quite the same experience or scenery that you can find while dolphin watching in Laos. First off, these dolphins are fresh water dolphins so you will be able to watch them in the Mekong River. These particular dolphins are believed to be responsible for saving the lives of travelers and locals who had trouble with the tough current found in this area. You can also see these dolphins at times around Don Khon.

While you are able to see the dolphins no matter what time of day you go, the locals will often recommend that you head out during the early morning or late in the afternoon. This is the time when the dolphins are the most active and many people aren't up and moving yet early in the morning so you won't have to fight with the crowds. Looking to get a bit more personal with the dolphins and see them up close? It is possible to charter a boat at Kong Ngay from the beach so you can get the best possible view of the dolphins on your trip.

Eastern Loop Hike

For those tourists who are ready to get up and walk in order to see the sights, or those who just love to hike, it is worth your time to take a visit to the Easter Loop Hike trail. This is a longer trail so make sure you are ready to go and wearing good walking shoes. This walk is going to take you down the eastern edge of the Don Khon area where the French once built concrete walls. You can take a look at the channels that were created in order to float logs from this area downstream so they could be used for other means. These walls are still present if you go on the Eastern Loop Hike and there is so much to learn about the history of the area if you have an afternoon free. You can also see some ancient bridges and walk through modern rice fields as well.

Elephant Riding

Nothing is quite like riding an elephant in the Champasak area. Not only will you really enjoy getting a chance to ride on one of these magnificent animals, you get to choose from a variety of trails. Take it easy and just go around the town, not far from your comfort zone. Or try something that you never thought possible by going into the jungle and seeing sights that aren't available in any other part of the world. There are several different groups you can go with and often feeding the animal, stopping for lunch, or seeing different sights are all some of the options that you can choose.

Laos Festivals

If you are able to work it out, you should make sure and visit Laos during some of their most popular festivals. There is nothing quite like the culture and fun of the Laos people and the best way to see all of this is by going during the festivals. The local people love to share some of this experience with tourists and you are sure to find some fun, as well as someone to explain some of the intricate details of the festival, no matter where you happen to be.

Most of the festivals in Laos are centered either around a Buddhist holiday or the agricultural season. The Lunar New Year is a good one to visit and it begins in mid-April. During this festival, you will notice that the whole country stops working and celebrates. Locals will clean their homes, many will visit their local temples to make offerings, and everyone will come together on the actual holiday to have a massive water fight all throughout the town. Think of how much fun it could be to walk into a random town during this time and just start a big water fight that everyone is a willing participant in? While this may sound like utter mayhem in some areas, it is all in good fun and a great way to bring in the New Year.

Another festival that you can check out is the Rocket Festival, or Bun Bang Fai, which happens in May. There is a lot of processions, dancing and music, and in the end there are bamboo rockets that are fired off. All of this is meant to come together to ask for rain for the crops.

For the most important festival of the year, you will want to visit during Bun Wat Phu Champasak. This festival is going to go on for three days and occurs during the full moon of the third lunar moon. There are a lot of activities that go on considering this festival lasts for three days and you can include things such as dancing, comedy shoes, cockfights, Thai boxing matches, and even boat racing.

No matter which festival you are able to attend, you are going to have a great time and get to meet some of the best people in this whole country. If you are able to schedule at the right time, make sure that you spend at least part of your vacation in Laos celebrating along with the people one of the great festivals of that area.

Railway Hike in Champasak

Do you have someone in your group who is fascinated by railroads and trains? Do you love to spend your vacations outside hiking around and getting to see as many of the wonderful sights that are available wherever you go? Do you just want to find something that everyone can enjoy and that is a bit off the tourist attraction path? Then take some time to visit the Railway Hike while you are in Champasak.

This hike is going to have you go about five kilometers down an old railway line through Don Det island. You are going to see a bit of everything when you go on this trek from villages, rice fields, and even the lush forest that Laos is known for. The end of the trek is a French pier that allows you to look over the water at Cambodia. If you do choose to go on this hike, make sure that you have good walking shoes and are an experienced hiker. The uneven land makes it really difficult to hike and biking is difficult.

Mountain Biking

While there are plenty of opportunities to go biking no matter where you go in Laos, you should take the time to visit some of the trails in Luang Prabang. There is just so much scenery that you are going to be able to enjoy in this area and whether you are a beginner or looking for something that is a bit more of a challenge, you can have a lot of fun in this area. Choose to go out on your own, although you will need to be careful since the terrain can quickly change, or go on one of the one day tours that will take you through the mountains, rural villages, across rivers, and all around this older town. These one day trips are designed with the beginner in mind so even if you haven't been on a bike in years, it can still be a really great experience. And of course, there are several bike tours that are meant for those who want a real challenge that will take you to more remote locations and even will have you crossing some rivers.

If you are interested in a different kind of biking tour, consider Spice Tours. This company has combined cycling and the culture of Laos into one. You will get on your bike and go down roads to a potter village where guests are allowed to spend some time, check out the wares, and even are served some of the local food. Most of the tours that you take will be about four hours, although check on this and see if you are able to go for the full length of the tour. The guide is able to speak English and all equipment and lunch is provided on the tours. Most groups do have limits so they don't get too large so make sure to book well in advance no matter which biking tour you would like to go on.

Hitting the River

Luang Prabang has the best location in almost the whole world for kayaking and rafting and there are plenty of tours that allow you to spend the day doing this activity. Whether you just want to give it a try or you want this to be your chosen mode of transportation to get from one location to another in the country, there is something for everyone.

For those who are a bit more experienced with kayaking, you should check out the Vietlong Travel tour when you are in this area. This is a challenge so beginners should pick something else, but you will be able to see a lot of great sights such as local tribes doing daily tasks, dramatic mountain landscapes, and higher intensity rapids. If you would like to take a trip that lasts for a few days, this is possible with the company Green Discovery Laos; this one allows you to spend the night with one of the hill tribe villages, cliff jumping, and so much more. Of course, there are some easier courses, some that may just take a few hours, that are better suited for beginners who may have never been in a kayak before so don't feel intimidated by some of these more challenging options.

Golfing at Luang Prabang

If your idea of a relaxing vacation includes playing a few rounds of golf, Luang Prabang has some of the best locations in all of the country. You not only get to play a challenging round of golf, but you get to have your pick of great backdrops to keep you entertained in between turns. Whether you want to look at the local town, the mountains, or the Mekong River, there is just so much to take in at this golf course. This golf course is about ten minutes from the middle of Luang Prabang and 15 from the local airport so it doesn't take long to get to at all. You can enjoy 18 holes of golf on a part 72 green. You can also just use the driving range, purchase something at the pro-shop to take home as a souvenir, or have a bite to eat at a five star Lao cuisine restaurant. There is just so much to enjoy and do at this location that you will feel like your time disappears quickly.

Bowling Alley in Luang Prabang

Ok, while this may not seem like something that you will really want to do when you're on vacation to a new and exciting location, it is a bit different than you may be thinking. While you are able to sit back and play a few rounds of bowling for a very affordable price, this is more of a night time hotspot where you can party, have a few drinks, meet some new people, and have a little fun. This area is known for attracting backpackers and tourists alike and it is a great place for you to have a night out on the town without having to break the bank on vacation. Try a few of the local specialties here and sit down and talk with some locals and other tourists that you may not meet anywhere else. This is a fun way to spend your night and you will be ready for another night of sightseeing when you're all done.

Spend an Afternoon at the Spa

No matter where you spend your time in Laos, make sure to visit the spa at least once when you're on vacation. Often doing this right when you first arrive can help to ease the tension and put you in the right frame of mind for actually enjoying your vacation and letting go of all the worries you had back at home. There are plenty of choices that you can go with and they fit all kinds of budgets. Some even offer a full body massage for just $5 and you can sit and relax in their onsite sauna when you're all done. There are some places that cost a lot more so watch out for this if you're on a budget.

Learn How to Weave and Dye

This is a huge pastime in the area of Vientiane. Many people thought that the ancient traditions of silk-weaving were lost when the Communist regime took over the area, but with some foreign influences and some interest from other countries, the people of this area have quickly gotten back into this industry. Spinning yarn is an important factor in the culture of Laos and you will often be able to see the women of the area weaving or working on another similar project. While in you are in the area, look around and see how this is all done. You can learn how to do the actual process just like the people of Laos do it today. In some areas, you can even take a class to learn how this is all done and have something unique of your very own to take home.

Swimming in Vientiane

While swimming may not seem like that big of a deal to many people in the world, it is one of the most popular activities, and one of the easiest to do, in the area of Vientiane. Some people choose to jump right into the Mekong

River, but this is not advised if you're not from the area and not a really good swimmer. The currents with this river can be really strong and many people have drowned because they are not used to how this river works. Rather than risking it at the Mekong, you should consider heading to some of the local swimming pools or resorts and making a whole day out of it.

If you are in the Vientiane area, you should check out the Settha Palace in order to really get a fun time swimming. This is a luxury resort that has a nice swimming pool for your group to enjoy and take in all of the surroundings. This will just cost $7 a day so very affordable considering all the things that you can do. You can also visit the Tai-Pan fitness center and swimming pool if you would like to make a day out of relaxing and getting a good workout. For those who would just like a quick swim or looking to really stay on a budget, the local public pool is nearby, and close to the Lao Plaza Hotel and the National Museum and only costs $1 for the day. Looking for something that children will enjoy and has some water slides and more fun? The new Nong Chan Water Park in this area is the best place to go and visit.

Houey Hong Vocational Training Centre for Women

This training center is located about seven kilometers from Vientiane in its own little village. It is surrounded by a nice little garden and there are about eight buildings present, some that are used as workshops and others that are more studios. This is a place for women of the area to learn more about the textile and weaving of the past. The funding of this center is pretty sporadic so the center is often on its own to keep open. In order to support itself, the center will sell crafts that the students make while also offering some tailoring services to the locals. There is also the chance to take a full or half day workshop so you can learn how to do some Loatian weaving including trial loom weaving, dyeing, tying thread, and designing patterns. If you have ever wanted to learn how to weave, this is the place to go to learn from the best. You get to take home your new creations and the costs of these workshops are going to include the materials, lunch, and the transfer to and from the area. It is really a great experience and for the cost, it is a good way to spend the day.

Dong Natad Trek

If you happen to be in the area of Savannakhet while in Laos, make sure to do the Dong Natad Trek. While this area is best known for all of its ecotourism spots, this trek is one of the best ones that you can choose from. You will start out this trek by going into the forest right outside of town. You will go past the Mekong Bridge and then near the salt mines. There is plenty of time to check out all the wild animals and birds and you will find that this is a nature lovers' paradise.

While you are on this trek, make sure to take a stop at the salt mines. You will learn a bit more about salt processing in this area. There is also areas that are considered sacred here and you can visit with the That Ing Hang Stupa, something that is a real treat after all this walking. You can do this in a one or two day trek and there really is something for everyone to see when you choose this option.

Temples in Laos

While you are in Laos, it is a good idea to check out some of the temples in the area. These temples are really beautiful to see and hold some of the most important parts of the history and culture of this area. Some of the best temples that you should consider visiting include:

- Pha That Luang—this is one of the most known landmarks in all of Laos. It is 45 meters high in the stupa and most believe that this area is holding a sacred Buddha relic. Of course no one is allowed up there so it is impossible to check, but the beautiful architecture as well as some of the history of this area will keep you occupied while you are there.
- Haw Pha Bang—This temple was built in order to enshrine the Phra Bang, one of the most highly venerated images of Buddha. This particular temple can be found in Luang Prabang on the grounds of the former Royal Palace. When you are done looking at this marvelous temple, take the time to walk the grounds and see just how peaceful this whole area can be.
- Wat Si Saket—this is the oldest temple in the area of Vientiane and all of it is still in its original form. This is really unusual in the area as most of the temples were destroyed during 1827. This whole temple is now a museum that holds more than 10,000 images of Buddha. For those who really want to see the history of Buddhism and want to see a traditional Laos temple that has not been updated or changed, this is a good place to start.
- Haw Phra Kaew—this particular temple received its name from the Emerald Buddha, the piece having been enshrined in this area until 1779. Now the temple is a museum that shoes 18th century Buddha images in bronze, ancient inscribed steles, and some of the other artifacts of this religion.
- Wat Inpeng and Wat Chan—these are some lesser known temples right by the Mekong River that can really help you see some more of the history of this area without having to fight all the crowds. These

temples are actually still active, but they do allow visitors to come and stop by. Since these temples are active, you need to be respectful when you are there. Dress in appropriate attire and take off your shoes before you enter into the temple.

These are just a few of the different temples that you will be able to find all throughout Laos. While these are some of the best, if you are able to come across any other temples in the area, go and see them. This country has a lot of neat history and the temples are some of the best places to see all of this.

The Buddha Caves—Pak Ou Caves

Going down the Mekong River is a great way to see a lot of the sights that are available in Laos. You are sure to spend quite a bit of your time in this area since many of the main attractions that you will want to see are available in this area. While you are near the Mekong River, make sure to make a stop with the Buddha Caves. These are really easy to get to from Luang Prabang just by taking a speedboat. You can spend quite a bit of time looking around at the sights, enjoying all that nature throws at you and you will enjoy all the religious background apparent by the Buddha images that are everywhere.

Plains of Jar

This is a really peculiar sight, but one you are not going to want to miss out on. These plains are located in Xieng Khouang and there are more than 400 of the sights, so you will find that this could take your whole day up if you want. The plains are full of rocks that are all over the terrain and some of these weight up to 6 tons each. This is a great sight if you just want to get out in the open and you want to see something that is unique and you won't be able to see anywhere else in the world.

No matter where you head throughout the great country of Laos, you are sure to find a lot of great things to see and do along the way. There are many great cities to visit, festivals to come and see, and a lot of great tradition that you will not be able to find anywhere else. Many people feel that this country is missing out on a lot because it is more landlocked compared to some of the others. But just a few days in this country, meeting all the nice people and having a good time, will show you that this is one of the best places in the world to spend your vacation. When planning your trip to Laos, make sure to include some of these stops along the way.

CONCLUSION

Laos is a great country to visit when you are ready to get out and relax. Whether you are doing a tour of all Southeast Asia or you want to spend your whole time in this area, you cannot go wrong with a good visit to Laos. The laid back culture, the great shops to visit, all the scenery between the mountains, river, and more, and even the outside atmosphere all bring together an experience that you will never be able to find somewhere else. This guidebook is the best companion that you need when it's time to get started with planning your ultimate Laos vacation.

CAMBODIA TRAVEL GUIDE

INTRODUCTION

The country of Cambodia is a great one for you to go visit. It has a lot of great history and you can spend some time visiting a country that has been lost in time and is finally able to reinvent itself after all this time. While Cambodia was pillaged for many years and under the rule of the French for some time, in recent years the country has been able to put in its own government and has been growing to allow more tourism and rebuilding to some of its older splendor.

If you have ever wanted to go to Cambodia and Southeast Asia, there is so much to do and see. And this guidebook is going to provide you with all the information that you need in order to prepare the best trip possible to this country. We will start out with a bit of the history of the country, talk about some of the ways to get a visa and to travel around the country, and move on to some of the fun stuff like good foods to eat, different ways to shop, and even the best places to visit while you are in Cambodia.

Whether you have been looking into going to Cambodia for a long time or are interested in finding the perfect place to vacation this year, this guidebook is here to help. You will learn the best places to visit and how to have the best time possible when you leave on your trip.

The History of Cambodia

Cambodia is a great stop to make on your global tour, but before you head out, there are a few things to remember. Cambodia is a poor country that has been down on its luck for many years now. While there are a lot of beautiful places that you can visit in this country, most of the people are going to have had some hard luck and you do need to be careful if you bring in any valuables to the country.

In 1431, the Angkor in Cambodia fell and the mighty Empire that was in place at that time started being plundered by everyone that is around them. In the 19th century, the French colonized the area and then in the 1970s, this area was heavily carpet bombed by the United States. In 1953, the country thought it was going to receive its own independence, but Cambodia was plunged back into a civil war in the 70s before seeing the reign of terror of Khmer Rouge. It wasn't until the UN stepped in and sponsored elections during 1993 that the country stood a chance to get back up on its feet.

With all of the things that happened over these years, the people of Cambodia were the ones to suffer. The country is still trying to get back on its feet and most of the people there are surviving on what is less than $1 USD each day. Being able to get their basic services is a bit spotty and there is still a lot of political intrigue that is going on in the country.

That being said, the security in this country has increased in recent years as the government has tried to increase their tourism in order to help out the people of the country. So visiting the country is pretty safe, you just need to remember the turbulent times that went on in this country and that a lot of the people are still trying to recover. Be polite and courteous and try to only bring the necessities when you visit this country and you should be just fine.

HISTORY

Cambodian history started long before the Khmer Rouge that has plunged it into the state that it belongs today. Before this time, the Cambodians had a triumphant history and they were one of the biggest and most magnificent states in that area. Once you see the temples of Angkor, you will be able to see how wealthy the Khmer Empire once was. The zenith of this empire came between 1181 and 1218 when the empire was able to make huge gains in territory from the Cham. At its height, Cambodia stretched into Vietnam, Laos, Burma, Malaysia, and Thailand, making it much larger than the area you would see now.

Once the Khmer Empire fell, Cambodia entered its dark ages. The Ankorian civilization started to use the Cambodia's water supply to help their own agriculture, leaving very little for the people of Cambodia. The Ayutthaya, the country that defeated Cambodia, spent the next 400 years taking from the people of Cambodia and they had to worry about their rivalries to the east and west of them.

Most historians felt that over this 400 years, Cambodia was basically going to disappear. There were just too many factions that were going against the people and they were never able to revive themselves. Many believe the fact that the French took over this colony was the main reason that they were able to continue existing.

While the French did take over this area, they were more interested in getting Vietnam and pretty much ignored the people of Cambodia except for the elite. These elite would eventually form the Red Khmers. During the Second World War, Japan gained a hold on Southeast Asia and undermined the goal of the French. Soon Prince Sihanouk declared the country of Cambodia as free, something that the French did not fight that much because they were still concentrating on making Vietnam their own at the time.

Prince Sihanouk became one of the main figures in Cambodia after this time. During his reign, there was more of an emphasis on education which would help the people finally take control of their country, as well as a huge Buddhist revival in the area. With this new educations, an educated elite arose and they were disenchanted with how few jobs were available in this area. No matter how hard they tried during this time, the economic situation in Cambodia would not get better and many of the newly educated young people became attracted to the Indochinese Communist Party and the Khmer Rouge.

Soon the Second Indochina War spread over to Cambodia and the United States became concerned with what was going on in that area. Their response was to send over the US Air Force and bombed the country from 1964 to 1973. This carpet bombing attempt is believed to have killed up to 150,000 people in addition to those who were killed from the war.

In 1970, Prince Sihanouk was taken from the thrown and Lon Nol, and other generals who the United States liked better, took over the thrown. Instead of just disappearing though, Sihanouk started to support the Khmer Rouge and many followed him. This group started to endear themselves with the rural poor, making them very much liked to the people who were tired of the way that things had been going for a long time.

Even though it took five years, the Khmer Rouge took over the Phnom Penh area and asked for an evacuation of all the towns and cities. It is believed that more than a million people died from enforced hardships and execution. Those in rural areas seemed to do better since they weren't in direct contact with the new government, but the Khmer Rouge extended its cruelty to everyone. Over the next few years, a genocide occurred in the country until the Vietnamese were able to drive out this government, ended 13 years of terror.

Because of all the harshness that the Khmer Rouge had put on the country, there was barely anything left to save. All commerce forms, money, and higher education had been destroyed and basically the country had to start up from scratch in 1978. There was finally a break in all of this turmoil when the UN sponsored some elections and helped to bring the country back to normal as well. In 1998, a new party came in and finally brought some political stability to the area when they were able to get the few Khmer Rouge forces to leave the area. At this point, the country is still trying to recover from all these years of turmoil and the people were looking for a government that would be able to help them out and get them out of this downward circle. With the new governments in place, the country was slowly rebuilding.

The economy of Cambodia is slowly starting to rebuild again and they are focusing their pillars on tourism and textiles. This is great news for you when you want to visit the country. It is estimated that almost 2 million tourists come into Cambodia each year to see the culture and the beautiful landscape. Over time, this country is looking to build up and hopefully they will be able to recover from the hundreds of years of wars, occupation, and other hardships they endured.

While this history is not full of majestic wins or big Empires over the past, there are still many great things to see. From the gorgeous beaches on one end to all the old temples that survived through the hard years, you are going to be able to find something for everyone when visiting this great country.

GETTING INTO CAMBODIA

Before heading over to Cambodia, you need to make sure you have the proper paperwork in place. Cambodia is very welcoming to tourists of all kinds and they understand that this is an important part of their economy and helping them to grow. That being said, you do need to make sure that you are getting the paperwork done to be allowed into the country before heading off on your vacation. Here are some of the things that you will need to get prepared for your great vacation.

VISAS

If you are from some areas in Southeast Asia, you will need to have a visa to come into Cambodia. This would include those who live in Vietnam, Thailand, Laos, the Philippines, Singapore, Malaysia, and Indonesia. The main tourist visa will just cost $30. If you are coming in to the country and trying to get a visa when you are at the boarders, stay firm on the price. There is still some corruption in the country and some of the staff is going to try to get you to pay more. If it is just a few dollars more, it is probably easiest to go with it, but if they are charging a lot more, you know it is a scam and stay firm on asking for the official price.

When you pick your visa, you can pick between a tourist and a business visa. As a traveler, the tourist visa is the best choice for you and it can be extended for up to two months if you need to stay in the country a bit longer. Business visas are for those who come to the country in order to work and these can be extended for a year or more.

The visas are obtained through the Cambodian consulates or embassies. You can get them on arrival at the major airports or the international border crossings, but it is often easier to get these visas before you even leave home to make your transition as smooth as possible. While the tourist visa is best for those who just want to come to Cambodia and have a nice vacation, if you feel that you are going to be staying in the country for more than two months, opt for the business visa to save problems down the line.

To apply for your visa, you will need at least two smaller photos that are recent as well as a passport, one or more page clear on your visa pages, some passport photocopies to give to the embassies when you arrive, and some US dollars to pay for the fees. There are also many steps that you will need to go through, plus some extra paperwork, if you wait until you get to the border, or the airports in Cambodia, to get your visa. Most tourists choose to purchase their visas online or through the mail before heading out. While these are going to cost a little bit more, they are going to save you a lot of hassle when you get to the country, help you to avoid talking to a lot of people and perhaps getting scammed, and allow you to get started on your vacation right away.

One option that is popular with visas is e-visas. These are a great way to go, especially if you are short on time and need to get the visa in right away. You will need to pay about $40, as of June 2015, and you need to send in a digital photograph that is recent. The visa will be sent back to you within 3 days and you are ready to go. If you do choose to go with this method though, make sure that you only purchase the e-visa through the Ministry of Foreign Affairs and International Cooperation. Any other site is most likely a scam and you will not get a true e-visa in this manner, causing problems when you get to Cambodia.

OVERSTAYING IN CAMBODIA

It is never a good idea to stay too long in Cambodia. If you are under 10 days over your visa when you make it to the immigration, it is possible to get off with just a little fine, but if you are caught by the police before you make it in, you will be sent to immigration and have long wait times. It is much better to get an extension of your visa rather than trying to dodge the system and hope you don't get caught. There are many agents that will be able to help you extend your visa, and they have streamlined the process so you won't have to wait too long before you are ready to stay in the country a bit longer.

Getting Around in Cambodia

Once you are in the country, there are a million things to see. You will be able to see a culture that is completely different than your own and has a great history. But choosing the manner that you will get around the country is an adventure all on its own. Some of the ways that you will be able to get around Cambodia include:

- Plane—there are many airports that operate passenger flights out of the major cities in the country. You can take these if you are planning on going from one end of the country to another.
- Helicopter—VIP helicopter charters are a great way to see some of the scenery that is around the country. You can see some of the sights from way up high. One popular flight is to go from Phnom Penh and Siem Reap and you can either go one way or two way with these flights. This is a great afternoon excursion that gets you high in the air and seeing so much.
- Roads—the government has been working hard in order to upgrade some of the roads through the country ever since 2008. This makes it easier than ever for you to travel around the country and get from town to town. You can share a taxi, rent out a truck, or take a bus to get to your next location.
- Boat—boats are a great way to see some of the beauties that Cambodia has to offer. There are ferries that operate during certain seasons and you can choose the major river that you like. This is also a very cost effective method because you will be able to get all the way from Phnom Penh to Siem Reap for just $33. This will take you about six hours to get to your location, although you will have to leave early in the morning. But along the way you can enjoy all the classic views of rural life and get a taste of something that you just have not been able

- to experience in the past. There are also luxury boats that cost more so you can find the method that is best for you.
- Train—while the passenger train system was shut down in 2009 and it is undergoing some major restorations, there are a few places where you can still travel by rail. There is about 111 km. that is between Touk Meas and Phnom Penh that offers a nice little ride while in the country. This spot is planning on eventually connecting with the railway networks in Vietnam and Thailand, but this has yet to be done.
- Go your own way—while many of the touring options above can offer you with something new and exciting to enjoy while on the road, you will still be able to take it your own way. Consider renting a car and having some fun with a guidebook to determine where you would like to go. Or you can take the time to try out a few of the different options to find the one that is best for you.

Remember that when you are traveling, no matter the method of transportation, you should respect to the people there. The bigger cities are used to the tourism and have adjusted, but some of the more out of the way cities have not adapted yet. Never take a picture or be disrespectful in any of these areas without asking the people first. Just like you wouldn't feel comfortable with someone coming into your yard and taking pictures, the people of rural Cambodia are not fond of it either.

While you are in this country, you will find that there are many great accommodations that you can enjoy. Most of the major towns are going to have places to stay that are much like the ones you would find in major cities across the western world. There are also guest houses and hotels in the rural parts as well. If you want just a basic guesthouse, it is possible to find a nice one that is $2 a night. In the city, the prices are going to be a bit higher, usually somewhere between $5 to $10 a night. Keep in mind if you would like something that is budget friendly, you will need to have your own amenities, including towels and such. The price for hot water and air conditioning can send the price up as well. There are also options for five star hotels in Cambodia that will cost you about $100 a night.

The Language of Cambodia

The official language in this country is known as Khmer. Unlike some of the countries that are all around Cambodia, this is not really a tonal language, although you may find that it is difficult to hear the differences. The Cambodians are able to speak a little bit of English, but they really enjoy it when tourists take the time to attempt their language, even if you are not the best with it. So grab a phrasebook before heading to this country and try out your skills with the language; you will make a lot more friends this way.

Learning how to spell all of the words in Khmer can be hard. There is no official spelling or symbols for each word, so it is not unusual to see the same word spelled in three different ways. You can either choose to bring along a translator, which is pretty cost efficient in these areas, or just learn how to pronounce some of the words. Be aware that there are also some different dialects of Chinese, Thai, and other languages spoken throughout the country so don't be surprised to hear some of these.

When you are looking at signs, you will notice that most of the big cities have placed signs in both English and in Khmer. In some cases, you will also see some signs in Chinese as well. This makes it a bit easier for you to get around if the spelling of a word does not make sense to you. In addition, most schools in Cambodia will teach some English so the people in major cities will be able to talk to you a little bit. Keep in mind most of the students just learn phrases though and aren't able to keep up a full conversation in English. Also, those who work in hospitality and tourism has some basic English knowledge, but if you start to get a bit off topic, they may not be able to understand you. Just keep in mind that they are new to learning English and be ready to repeat yourself to get some help.

One thing to watch out for is the body language of the people that you are talking to. Instead of asking you to repeat what you said all of the time, many Cambodians will smile, nod curtly, and then look the other way when they aren't able to understand you. They feel that this is the best way to avoid embarrassment of either party, but they really don't understand what you are asking. Find another way to ask the question or consider bringing along a translator to ensure everything goes smoothly.

While there is a lot of culture and this society was kept away from English speaking countries for a long time, there are still many people who will be able to help you out when you're in Cambodia. Just be patient and perhaps learn a few words or phrases in Khmer and you will find it is much easier to get around.

Staying Safe in Cambodia

For the most part, you are not going to have any trouble staying safe when you are in Cambodia. The government has done a great job at helping to make this country safe for all of the tourists that come in and out. But, just like with any country, when you get into the big cities, you will have to be careful about some safety concerns and theft. These are problems that occur in most of the cities in Cambodia, but especially in Phnom Penh. The best thing that you can do is be really discreet about the items that you are carrying around and never go out late at night, especially in those dark and secluded areas, on your own.

While in the country, consider bringing your own lock and keys for anything that you are going to store, such as valuables or even a bike if you plan to rent one out for the visit. There are some rental staff that may make extra keys and steal your items when you aren't nearby to watch. With your own lock, which is easy to use at any of the rental places, you will be able to rest knowing your items are safe. This is advice you can follow no matter where you go on a trip.

CRIME

When visiting Cambodia, remember that the laws in Cambodia are not always the most enforced. The country is still working on rebuilding and often you will need to resort to bribery to get anything investigated. There is also a lack of police force in the tourist areas so you are going to be kind of on your own when you are in Cambodia. That being said, for the most part, it is pretty safe in the country. You will find that the violent crime rate is pretty low, and this is even more for foreign visitors. If you use your common sense and don't try to show off your valuables or act rude to the people of the country, you really have nothing to worry about while visiting Cambodia.

STAYING HEALTHY

When you are in Cambodia, you should take some caution to be careful everywhere you go. Unlike some of the more developed countries, Cambodia does not have the medical facilities or personnel that you may expect in case you get hurt. The further away you are form the cities, the harder it is to find the doctors and other medical tools that you need in order to stay healthy. So while you are in Cambodia, it is a good idea to try and stay healthy and don't get seriously injured while you are on the trip.

If you have a serious medical concern when you are in the country, it is best to go to Singapore, Ho Chi Minh City, or Bangkok if you are anywhere near this area. They have the best services for those who can afford them. The Royal Phnom Penh Hospital is a good one to go to as well, but the costs can get a bit expensive if you don't have the right insurance. Make sure that your insurance plans are updated and that they are willing to cover you if you have an accident overseas.

The hospitals and other clinics that are in local rural areas vary a lot for how good of service you will receive. Some of them are fine if you get a little cut, but won't be able to handle bigger health issues. Other clinics can provide frightening care as many of the doctors may not be fully certified, the clinics will have poor equipment, and often will give out either old medicines or placebos in their place. If you are in a rural area, it is best to be extra careful or avoid going in as much as possible or you could end up with worse problems than before.

Before heading to Cambodia, go and visit your doctor and make sure that you are up to date on all of your vaccines. While the Cambodian government doesn't require you to have certain vaccinations or a health certificate, unless you are from Africa, this is more for your own safety. Most doctors will recommend that you get a polio booster, meningitis, hepatitis B, diphtheria, and tetanus just to be on the safe side. Also, bring along plenty of bug spray as the mosquitos in the area can be nasty.

Many tourists choose to bring some of their own medical kit supplies into Cambodia with them. This allows them to provide some basic first aid, which is all you should need while you are traveling. If you are planning on bringing a kit, keep some insect repellant (dengue from mosquitos are common), scissors, bandages, calamine lotion, oral rehydration solutions, and some antibiotics.

Dehydration can happen to some tourists who don't plan things out well ahead of time. Make sure that you need to take in at least 2 liters of water each day, although more is best if the weather is hot and you are moving around a lot. Don't drink any untreated water or water products no matter what country you go into to ensure you stay healthy. You may want to avoid traveling to Cambodia during March and April as these are the hottest months and can make you feel miserable or bring on dehydration more than ever. If you do travel in this time, make sure to bring a lot of water, wear a hot, and keep the sunscreen nearby.

While you are in Cambodia, you should be pretty safe when it comes to your health, as long as you make sure that you are healthy before heading out and take precautions before you go out on a hike or on your adventures. Most tourists report that the country is safe, but be careful when you are out and choose your hospital wisely when you do need the assistance.

MAKING PURCHASES IN CAMBODIA

The Cambodian riel is the currency of choice in this country. It is pretty much interchangeable with the US dollar in most places. You may want to keep a few of the riel on hand with you when traveling in Cambodia. While a lot of the big cities will take the US dollar for your purchases, this is not something that has extended to the rural areas and you will find that it is difficult to make purchases there without the right currency.

Most of the cashiers that you will encounter want the bills to be in almost perfect shape. Some tourists have complained that a cashier would not accept a bill because there was a small rip in it, regardless of whether the bill was a US dollar or a riel. Usually some clear tape can help fix this up or just bring newer bills along with you.

If you take your US dollars to Cambodia and try to exchange them, the current exchange rate is 4000 riel per dollar. There are some businesses that will charge you a bit more for the services of exchange so be careful about where you are getting this done. In addition, you should exchange back all the riels when you are done back to your US dollars as these don't have any value once you leave Cambodia and even more banks outside the country will not exchange these.

For the most part, there are plenty of ATM's that you can visit throughout the country, whether you are in the cities or somewhere out in the middle of nowhere. Just to be safe, stop at one in a big city and make sure that you have enough money to make it through until you can get back.

Using Cards

It is becoming more common for travelers to take their credit cards overseas with them in order to make purchases without carrying money around. Before leaving your home country, make sure to alert the banks that you are going to be gone and for how long you plan to be out of the country. Failure to do so can result in the card being declined because your bank will assume someone is using is fraudulently. In addition, make sure to keep your eyes on your card at all times. These cards are easy to lose and then you can be stuck in Cambodia without any money.

Right now, JCB and VISA are widely accepted throughout the country and you will be pretty safe using these options. American Express and MasterCard are gaining in popularity, but there are still plenty of areas that won't use these options. VISA cards will usually have a limit of $1000 USD so be careful how much you are taking out at a time.

While more and more businesses are starting to take credit cards, most tourists will find these are used mostly to take money out of the ATM. Budget accommodations and restaurants are not going to take any type of credit card and there are a lot of stores in rural areas that are not set up to take these cards either.

Shopping

When you are shopping in Cambodia, you should make sure to watch out for signs that say Heritage Friendly Business Logo. The Heritage Watch was launched in order to support the development, heritage, culture, and arts in Cambodia. Businesses that give back to their local communities will be certified with this logo. This helps you to pick out businesses that are not only trustworthy but which also are working to help out their communities.

It is strongly advised that tourists do not purchase anything from children sellers no matter where they are located throughout the country. There are many adults who will send their children out to sell trinkets or to bag, often late at night or putting them in locations where predators may lurk. This is unsafe for the children and there are government organizations that are working to get these children off the street and to help the families out with their issues. You may also run into this problem with women carrying babies, old women, disabled people, and even more.

Don't feel like you need to help out these people, even though your humanitarian heart may say otherwise. Any area that is really desolate and needs some help has plenty of government aid all around. And even in those areas that don't have these options, the children are going to be supported by their families, even if this includes distant relatives. Families help each other out in Cambodia and often the children are sent out more to make some extra money on the side rather than the fact that they are desolate for the money.

When you are shopping, stick to areas that have nice stores and are in more common areas. Stay away from peddlers and others who may try to trick you out of money or with fake objects. Some markets are nice, but bring along someone else to ensure that you stay safe and learn the art of haggling so you get the best deal.

Haggling

Haggling is a great pastime that you can enjoy while in Cambodia. In fact, you can see success no matter where you haggle in the country. Rates for your apartments or guesthouses, outdoor food stalls, the products that you buy as gifts, and so on are often negotiable to a seasoned haggler. You do need to be careful; if the Cambodian feels that they are being cheated in a haggling situation and aren't getting a good deal, it is common for them to explode and not want to work with you any longer. Some things that you should keep in mind when you start haggling include:

- Be sensitive and considerate when you are haggling.
- There are many items that are fixed price, especially if they are not meant for tourists. Basically, food and tourist attractions can be haggled, but things you would get at a grocery store or other necessities usually are not.
- Sit down restaurants will usually not allow haggling so save this for outside vendors.
- Haggle in a group. If you have a few people who are with you to haggle, it is easier to get the Cambodian to agree with you.
- Talk to the boss. It is much easier to haggle for a better price when the boss is involved.
- Avoid full price near the Angkor temples. These are usually tourist traps and they are often willing to go down quite a bit.
- Be careful with haggling for moto drivers near where you plan to stay during the vacation. They will watch out for your safety more if they feel you are a good customer rather than when you are mean to them and haggle their prices too much.

The best place to haggle in Cambodia is Siem Reap so if you are in this area, you can get some great deals on your shopping. Phnom Penh is another good areas as well. You can usually tell where you will be able to get a good deal or where you should just go with the asking price based on the establishment you are in.

EATING

Compared to some of the other cuisine in Southeast Asia, you will find that this is great food that is cheap and filling, making it easier for the traveler to get some great meals without blowing their whole budget. The traditional Khmer food has started to go out of style, thanks to the fact that the era of the Khmer Rouge wiped out most of the Khmer cuisine, but there are still some great options. Some of the best options that you can try out when you are in Cambodia to get a taste of the traditional include:

- Amok—this is one of the most popular dishes in Cambodia. It is made with some shrimp, fish, and chicken along with vegetables and served inside a coconut with some rice on the side.
- K'tieu—this is basically a noodle soup but will be served during breakfast. Meat is the main ingredient but you can choose from fish sauce, sugar, chili powder, or lime juice for a flavoring.
- Somlah Machou Khmae—this is a sweet and sour soup that has fish, tomatoes, and pineapple inside. It is usually sold warm with some fresh noodles.
- Bai Sarch Ch'rouk—this is another staple of breakfast that includes picked vegetables, pork meat, and some rice.
- Saik Ch'rouk Cha Kn'yei—this is pork that has been fried with some ginger and it is easy to find in almost any location.
- Lok lak—this is chopped beef that is served with a dipping sauce of onion, lettuce, black pepper, and lime juice. Chips are often served on the side.
- Mi/Bai Chaa—this is just fried rice or noodles.
- Trey Ch'ien Chou 'Ayme—this is fish that has been fried with vegetables and sweet chili sauce.

- K'dam—if you are looking for some seafood, this is a good option. This dish is basically crab that is cooked with black pepper.
- Pong Aime—this translates to sweets but you will be able to choose from a variety of them from many street vendors and come with sugar water, condensed milk, and ice.
- Tuk-a-loc—this is a blended drink that includes ice, condensed milk, egg, and fruits.

If you are out and about and looking for something that is tasty for dinner that will also provide you with some of the best of Cambodian culture, these are some great dishes that you have to try out. You can find these at some of the local establishments or even at many street vendors so there are many opportunities to find something amazing.

DRINKS

While you are in Cambodia, you need to make sure that you have some of the tasty drinks that are available. Of course, make sure that you bring along some water purification tablets. The water is not always considered the freshest in this area and bottled water companies have grown quite a bit in the past few years in the country. If you eat at a restaurant and have some water, this is generally safe, but if you purchase something from a street vendor or use water on your own out in the wild, you will need to be careful. Here are some of the different options that you can have with drinks include

Soft Drinks

First is iced coffee. This is freshly brewed with some condensed milk. Any eatery that you find throughout the country will be able to provide this for you to enjoy and many of the locals like to sit down and have one while talking to friends. You will be able to get an iced coffee for about $4.

Iced tea is also popular and many times it is going to have some sugar and fresh lemon to give it a great new taste. You will love this after a hard day traveling through the country and looking for new attractions.

Fresh coconut is a safe and sanitary drink to have when you take it from the coconut. Most of the locals will drink the coconut juice from some plastic bags, but you can talk to your server and get help if you would like a new experience to just drink it straight from the coconut.

Alcohol

Right now, there is no legal drinking age in Cambodia, although this is becoming a concern for the government thanks to many children going on drinking adventures and becoming hurt. Most Cambodians are not casual drinkers and when they go out to drink, they plan to get wasted and have as much fun as possible right away. Drinking is considered a male activity because the rowdiness that comes from drinking a lot pretty quickly is not a good thing for virtuous women in the country.

Rice wine and palm wine are popular, but if you are getting them from a local seller, you may want to be careful about how sanitary they may be. Anchor is a great option because it is a cheap beer that tastes amazing and you will see that it is able to get you drunk pretty quickly. Golden Muscle Wine is advertised everywhere and doesn't taste that good when you drink it straight, but add it to some cola or tonic water, and you have a drink that is fun for a night on the town.

If you are going out with some friends that you made in Cambodia, be careful about what you are doing. Cambodians like to go out with friends and egg them on, and you could end up taking on more than you can handle, making it difficult for you to say no while getting too drunk at the same time. Take someone you can trust along with you and learn the best way to say no when you are done.

Eating out and having some of the local drinks in Cambodia is one of the best ways that you will be able to really learn about the culture and have a lot of great fun at the same time. Make sure to try out at least a few of the local dishes to find out just what is enjoyed in the country and perhaps you will learn some of your new favorites at the same time.

THINGS TO SEE IN CAMBODIA

So now that you know a lot of the basics and fun things about Cambodia, it is time to bring out this guidebook and learn about all of the fun things to see in Cambodia. Even though this country was plagued with a lot of hardships for many years, there are still a lot of things that you will be able to enjoy about this country. Some of the ancient artifacts, temples, and even some great places to hang out on the beach are all available in Cambodia. There is something for everyone. Let's take some time to look at all the fun things you will be able to see and do when you are in Cambodia.

Get on a Tuk Tuk

The first thing that you should do when you are in Cambodia is get on a tuk tuk. These are top of the line in Cambodia and they can be a lot of fun. Think small cushioned chariots that are going to take you around the city, or a specific area, by someone who is on a motorbike. You basically get to sit back and have some fun while watching all of the things that are going on. Whether you choose one to go on a tour or you are looking for a quicker way to get from one place in the city to another, these are the best options for keeping you nice and cool in the heat and to try out something that is really unique.

While walking is a popular activity for a lot of the tourists that go through Cambodia, a tuk tuk can change things up a bit. These are pretty affordable and can be a nice break from all the heat that is around most of the year in Cambodia. Plus, this is much faster if you are in a hurry to get to your next location or if you just have a lot to see during the day. Even if you don't feel that it is necessary, go on at least one tuk tuk ride to get the full experience of living in this area.

Go to Foreign Correspondent's Club

This club is in Phnom Penh, a city that you will need to spend at least a few days in when you head to Cambodia, and you will be able sit back and watch the Mekong River. If the day is too hot for you to get out and do as much as you would like, the balcony on this club is the perfect place to go. The breeze will feel amazing and you are going to just be able to take a nice break from all of the other things that you have done that day. The food is also pretty good so consider going out for supper where you can enjoy a nice cold drink, half off during supper time, and just enjoy yourself after a long day of sight-seeing.

Rabbit Island

Rabbit Island is a small little place that is right off the Cambodian coast. This island has a lot of thick jungle around it, but you will really enjoy the quiet and sandy beaches that are lined with hammocks and coconut trees. Whether you are looking for a fun day at the beach to take it easy after all the traveling or you would like to stay on the beach, at one of the affordable bungalows that are provided there, you are sure to have a great time no matter what you do while there.

For those who would like to take some time to go around the thick forest, make sure that you bring along a tour guide. They will be able to help you find the right spots to visit in the area and will make sure that you aren't going to get lost. For most people to head over to Rabbit Island, going out to the beach and just relaxing is one of the best activities and you can enjoy doing this as well.

Eat some Crab at Kep

Crab is a great dish to eat when you are in Cambodia. It is fresh right from the river so it is better than what a lot of people are able to enjoy in other parts of the world. This is so fresh, that in some areas, such as in the area of Kep, you will be able to reach into the ocean and then get all the crab fresh for your table.

While you are able to get some crab anywhere in the country, the place that is the most famous for their crab is Kep. This area is about four hours of driving from the major town of Phnom Penh, but you will not regret it. In fact, watching your dinner be prepared is an experience in itself. In many cases, as soon as you order your meal, the servers will go out to the shore and pick out the crab from their traps that will be part of your meal. This is a lot of fun for kids to watch as they guess which of the crabs will be on their dinner plate.

Visit a thrift store

In particular, go and visit one of the Sakura Japanese stores. These are not locations that everyone is going to enjoy a lot, but if you want to get a great bargain on the things that you purchase while shopping, or you like vintage clothes, this is the place that you need to see. They are located in most of the big cities, although they are a bit hidden compared to the other areas, but you will find that they are really interesting and anything fashion related is great. Many of the items are $0.25 so you are really getting some good deals.

There are a lot of thrift stores available in this area, and you just need to look around. Since the people in this area are often living on $1 a day, finding places were goods and services are cheap and easy to purchase is not too difficult. These thrift stores will work much like what you will be able to find at home; you can receive quality goods for a fraction of the price that you will pay somewhere else and have all the gifts that you need to bring home to friends.

Eat some Amok

A trip to any country is not complete until you take the time to eat some of their local fair. This allows you to have the time eating something that is new and unusual to you, but gives you a look into the lives that the citizens enjoy around you. Amok is one of the most popular dishes and it tastes the best when you purchase it right from the source. This is basically a kind of curry that is made with coconut milk, lemon grass, and some sort of meat. Sometimes there is a secret ingredient in, but each vendor has their own ideas and they want to keep this secret. You will be able to enjoy this with some rice or a coconut and it is very tasty.

Not only is Amok a great dish that people can enjoy in Cambodia, but there are quite a few others that can be amazing as well. Try out as much of the local food as possible when you visit Cambodia. You can choose from these options either at the restaurant that you are visiting or consider going to a street vendor for some other options. Tasting the foods that are available in a certain area can help you to learn more about the culture and can also be a lot of fun.

Visit the Archaeological Park in Angkor

This is the number one attraction for tourists in all of Cambodia and the government spends a lot of time advertising this place because it makes them a lot of money. But you should take the time to go and visit this park and see what all the fuss is about. This park is located inside Siem Reap and you will be able to see the temple ruins from years ago. Remember the history that we talked about earlier in this guidebook? The temples from the golden days of Cambodia are still preserved in this park and you will be able to go through all of them. Make sure that you grab a guide with you to help learn a bit more as you go and perhaps consider going on a tuk to make it easier to get around the whole place. This is going to be a hot and sweaty day, but you can learn about the history in this area so much better than anywhere else.

If you would like to tour these areas in a really unique way consider doing a helicopter ride over the ruins or even riding an elephant through the areas. This can allow you to see all the beauty that it has to offer in a way that many people would not even dream about.

Visit the Phnom Penh National Museum

This national museum has everything that you would want to see to show the history of this great country. It is filled with many ancient sculptures and statues that were taken out of the Angkor Temples. The idea was to remove these artifacts to help protect them from others who might try to touch them and ruin them or even scavengers who would steel them. In addition to seeing all the great artifacts, you will be able to see the great architecture of the building itself as well as the sweet garden and the fish pond that are right in the middle. If you are going to be here, plan on spending a few hours or more to get the full feel.

Go to the Sihnoukville Beach

No vacation is complete without spending some time at the beach. While this one might not be as famous as some of the ones in nearby Thailand, this is still a really nice beach that you can get out and enjoy to have a day off or just for something fun to do on a day off. The beaches have a lot of great lounge chairs that are ready for you to use and the beaches are really clean so you won't have to worry about all of this. There are plenty of restaurants that are ready to take care of any hunger needs you may have. It is also possible to get onto one of the local boats and see some of the other islands nearby or go snorkeling as well.

Get a Massage

This is not just any massage. It is possible to get a great massage while you are sitting on the beach. There are a lot of locals who are on the beach, ready to give you the royal treatment if you so choose. You can get anything from a massage, your nails done, and so much more. These are usually pretty cheap and can make your visit to the beach much better. Make sure to not take any of the services offered by children though. This is illegal in Cambodia and the kids should be in school anyway.

There are a lot of great places to get a massage. Some places are located on one of the beaches or you can head to a professional massage therapist building in one of the bigger towns along the way. There are a lot of places that will offer professional services that you will really like and are even better than what you can find at home. The best part is the price is even better than what you will find in most other countries, so it is easier than ever to pamper yourself while you're on vacation.

Get on an Ibis Bus

In order to get around Cambodia, you may have to get on one of the buses that are available. This can save you a lot of money compared to flying around and can give you a great ride. The best one for you to try out is the Giant Ibis Bus Services. This is a luxury bus company that is new, clean, and spacious and can also provide you with free Wi-Fi so you can have some fun on the trip. They are only $1 more compared to the other bus companies so you are getting a great deal compared some of your other options.

See the Fish Doctor

This is a great experience if you are bringing along younger children and want them to have some fun. When you visit the fish doctor, you will go into a room that has a huge tub filled full with fish. You and the other people in your party will place your feet into the tank and let the fish nibble any of the dead skin that is there. This is relaxing to some and a great experience for others. Either way, it is something that you won't be able to find anywhere else so it might be worth your time.

If you are taking your children to the fish doctor, make sure that they are comfortable with the idea. Some children like the idea of being able to get their toes wet and have little fish come and slide all over them, and other children are going to find this appalling. You will have to listen to your children and determine if this is the right step for you to take during the vacation. Or if someone in your group doesn't feel comfortable with the idea, consider doing something else instead.

See a Central Market

There are many markets all throughout the country for you to visit, so if you aren't able to spend as much time in Phnom Penh, you will be able to catch up on the market scene later on. But the central market in this city is one of the best and has a lot of special things that you will enjoy. To start with, the building that houses the market is built in a 1930s art deco style so that is something that is really fun to see. All of the markets are for bargain shoppers so no matter what you are trying to find, you will be able to get it for a good price when you go to the Central Market.

Learn some of the history

If you are interested in learning more about the history of Cambodia or have a history nut in the group, you should take some time to visit the S21 Museum and the Killing Fields. S21 was at one time a school in Cambodia that was changed into a torture chamber and a prison during the time of Khmer Rouge. This showed that despite the fact that the country had been trying to rebuild itself once being freed from France, it had quickly gone downhill when the Khmer Rouge appeared and even the schools were no longer valued. The site is still very much the same as it was during the Khmer Rouge and many people were brought to tears when they visited here. The people have kept this place open to show their people and the tourists the horrible things that happened in the past.

Once you are done visiting this museum, you may want to spend some time at the Killing Fields. This is an area that is a bit out of town. The Khmer Rouge was a rough group that killed thousands of people throughout the years and often this was done in the Killing Fields. Hundreds of thousands of people were killed and then buried in these fields. In modern times, it has been turned into more of a memorial site so you are able to wander around while learning about this trying time in history.

Go to a Movie

Even in Cambodia, it is possible to have a night out on the town and see a movie. The Flicks Community Movie House is one of the best places to visit when you are in Phnom Penh. This is a smaller location, holding about 32 people when it reaches capacity, but you will still get to watch the movies on a huge screen. Rather than always seeing the latest blockbusters coming up on the screen, you will get a nice variety between new and old films so you can always be on your toes about which movie is out. This is a nice way to take a break from all the sightseeing because you can cozy up in a small area and watch a movie, just like at home.

This is a cozy place for you and others in your family to relax after going through and seeing all the other sites that this country has to offer. Perhaps if you're in a large group you and your spouse can head out to a movie for a night out away from the kids. No matter why you head out to the movies, this is the one place that you should go and visit because of the cozy atmosphere and how much fun it can be to see some of your old favorite movies.

Visit Lake Tonle Sap

For those who are staying in the area of Siem Reap, it is worth your time to go and visit Lake Tonle Sap. This is just a little drive from the area and is the largest fresh water lake in all of Southeast Asia. It provides more than half of the fish that are consumed throughout Cambodia and you will also notice a lot of other peculiar things that are going on in the area. There are floating villages right on the lake, large bird colonies, and a huge snake population; the locals are able to catch more than 4 million snakes in this lake each year. It is definitely a sight to go visit when you are in the area.

If you are a bit queasy with the idea of snakes, you should find somewhere else to go. While this is a really pretty lake, the snakes are going to be pretty much everywhere and this could turn a lot of tourists away from this area. It may be best for families to just spend an hour or so by this lake and then head over to one of the other beaches throughout the country in order to get some relaxation and fun in the sun.

The Orussey Market

This is another market that you should take the time to visit when you are in the major city of Phnom Penh. It is always full of activity and it is the location that most of the locals are going to go in order to purchase the wares that they need. Whether you are looking for some dried food or some hardware to bring home, as well as anything in between, there is something for everyone at this market. This market is inside, so you can get out of the heat, and there are several levels that have hundreds of stalls. This is a market full of authentic items, so if you want to get something that is really unique to the area and that no one else has, this is a great option for you to go with.

Ta Prohm

If you are a fan of the Tomb Raider series of movies, you need to spend some time visiting the Ta Prohm. This is an area that is really fun to see and was the inspiration for the movies so you will see a lot of things that you will recognize. The temple was left exactly as the people found it so you will get the authentic experience including the crumbling walls with tree roots. The rest of the temples in the area were found in much the same way, but it is still a great place to go and visit.

This is a large area so make sure that you take some time to see everything. You will be able to see a lot of the history that came about during the Khmer dynasty, long before things went downhill for this country, and see just how great the culture in this area is. You will want to take the camera so that you are able to get some of the best pictures around these temple pieces.

Sunset Tour

This is the tour that you have to go on when you are in the Siem Reap area. You will take the tour on ATVs that go through some rural dirt roads. You will need to have good control over your driving before going on this trip. While it is a lot of fun, the unpaved roads are a little bumpy for some that are not used to the whole thing. But when you reach the end, you will get to look at a great scene that is not possible anywhere else. This is the sunset through the rice paddies. You will get to stay there until the sun is gone, and you are sure to have a lot of pictures taken from this site. If you would like to get on this tour, make sure to get started early because it is popular.

The Sunset Tour is one that everyone on your family will be able to enjoy. While you are going to head off road for a little bit, you will find that the road is pretty simple to be on and those who run the business really have a great idea of what they are doing. You can let the leaders know about your personal preferences and experience with riding so you won't get yourself into a situation that is uncomfortable or unsafe for you. Bring along the whole family and enjoy yourself on the ATVs while watching a beautiful view of the sunset that you won't be able to find anywhere else.

Siem Reap Night Market

Looking for a way to get out on the town when you are in Cambodia, the Night Market in Siem Reap is the best option. There are a lot of places to eat, party, and have a lot of fun. You can also get some great deals on some products that you would like to purchase and bring back home. You are going to feel like you are back home in New Orleans during the Mardi Gras season with just a bit of time in this area. Just make sure to bring some friends because it is easy for the partying to get out of control.

This is the best place to stop if you want to have a night out on the town. There is just so much that you are going to be able to do in order to have fun when you go out for this kind of thing, but when you are in Siem Reap, you have to spend at least one night out enjoying everything that the city has to offer. Whether you go out to one of the local taverns and have a few drinks, be careful when going with some of the locals to avoid trouble but do take some time to try out a drink that you aren't able to taste at home, or you want to check out some fun stores that are only open at night, you are going to find a ton to love when you go to the Night Market in Siem Reap.

Eat some bugs

This is another thing that the adventurous traveler will be able to enjoy when they are in Cambodia. You can stop right on Route 6 and have a try of some bugs and spiders, and other fare including birds, crickets, and tarantulas, and go home to tell all your friends that you tried something new. This is not for the faint of heart so skip it if you don't want the children to jump on it and try to eat all the bugs. But it can be a great experience for your group if you want to try out something new that everyone hasn't been able to try back at home. If only one person in your group is brave enough to try the insects, there are some mangos and bananas available for the rest who do not want to eat them.

Kbal Chhay Waterfall

No trip to Cambodia is completed without taking time to go and see some of the beautiful waterfalls that are all throughout this country. And the Kbal Chhay Waterfall is a great one to visit. This waterfall is right at the end of a big lake and will take a bit of time to get to since it's a little bit out of the way. Many of those who have gone to visit this waterfall suggest getting a scooter to reach the waterfall as the path is going to take some time to hike. Bring a nice picnic with you because this is the perfect place to go when you just need a break from it all, are looking for something with a lot of great scenery, and you just want to enjoy some time with family.

If you are traveling to Cambodia during a public holiday, you may want to keep away from these waterfalls during those special days. The citizens of Cambodia like to go and spend the day at the Kbal Chhay Waterfall so you will find that it is really packed and not as much fun to go and visit with all these people. But most days of the year, this is a more secluded area that can be a great get away with your family.

The Golden Lions

While you are in the bustling city of Sihanoukville, take some time to go and visit the Golden Lions. While some tourists feel like this is not worth the hype, there is a lot to love when it comes to visiting this monument. First, the statues are really large and can be fun to see how they were constructed. Many people stop here on their journey to get a picture and to explore the area that is all around the Golden Lions. This is ranked in the top 5 places to visit while in the city, and much of this has to do with the night life, restaurants, and other fun things to do right by the statues.

Wat Leu Temple

The Wat Leu Temple is located in Sihanoukville and is one of the main Wats in this town. These are Buddhist temples that are scattered throughout the city and are one of the main reasons that tourists come to this area. This particular Buddhist temple is in the perfect place for visitors to get a view of pretty much everything. You will be able to enjoy the beautiful mountains, just 6 kilometers away from the little temple and since Sihanoukville is a port city, you will also be able to look out at the sea and notice the tiny islands that dot the horizon.

Take some time to walk around the temples and take in the sounds and the sights. Be respectful though; this is a place of worship and the main part of the temple is usually reserved for the monks and tourists will not be allowed. Ask questions about the area and learn some more about how great Cambodia is and about their religious culture as well. You can easily get lost in the architecture and other wonderful things that are found inside this temple and many who go to visit state that they feel some inner peace when done.

The Snake House

While you are in the town of Sihanoukville, take a stop to the Snake House. This is the perfect place for anyone who has an interest in snakes and other reptiles or a fun little stop if you have some children you are bringing along. Don't worry though, there are a lot of different animals that you can enjoy outside of snakes including monkeys, birds, and crocodiles so it is similar to visiting a zoo. This is a great family outing with all of the room to walk around, the animals that your kids and family will love. While there, make sure to try out some of the food. There are options from local fair to Russian fair so you should be able to find something that will work for everyone.

Syn Absinthe Distillery

This is really a treat for any tourist who had never gone to Cambodia but who would like to try something that is new and original. There are tours available at this distiller each day around 3 so you are sure to be able to fit this into any of the plans you have while in Cambodia. You will be able to learn how the Cambodians make their most famous drinks, Absinthe, and take home some samples for the whole family. Not only can you see how the distilling process works, but you will learn a bit more about how absinthe works and even how it can help to aid in digestion, if taken in small amounts, and promotes lucid dreaming. Take off an afternoon for this truly unique visit that can be a lot of fun.

Stray Dog Adventures

Stray Dog Adventures started in 2005 and is one of the premier trips to take when you are in Sihanoukville. If you are looking for something that is completely different than what you will be doing in any other vacation and you want some adventure, this is the place for you. The Stray Dog Adventures is all about going for a thrilling as well as unique adventure through Cambodia, mostly by traveling on dirt bikes and going off road. You will be able to choose from a variety of options including going across the elephant mountain ranges, by some white and sandy beaches, seeing rural villages and hill tribes, and even going to some of the ruins that are popular for tourists.

When choosing this option, just make sure that you pick the right skill level for you. They offer tours from those who have never been on a dirt bike all the way up to those who are more advanced. You can also choose from a pretty laid back scenic look at the country or push it to the limit with something that is more extreme. If you want to go and enjoy this fun activity, and see the country in a way that you have never seen it before, the Stray Dog Adventures is the way to get this done. It is best to go sometime between November to April in order to avoid the rainy season, but other than that you are going to have a lot of fun on this trip.

Buddy Land Water Park

The Buddy Land Water Park is a good stop to make when you need a break in the afternoon and have young children. They are sure to have a lot of fun with the inflatable options and everyone in the party will be able to cool down from all the heat that is prevalent in Cambodia. You probably won't spend a ton of time in this area, but it is still a lot of fun for the kids to splash around in between traveling trips or just for something to do on a lazy day in the town. Going down the slide for the afternoon will only cost a few dollars so it is great for the budget traveler or as something to just throw into the trip at the last minute.

Cambodian Children's Painting Projects Gallery

If you are in the area and want to help out a great cause in Cambodia, you should visit the Cambodian Children's Painting Projects Gallery. This is an area where local children can showcase their own personal artwork for others to see and many of them are available to purchase. Even if you just want to walk around and see some of the artwork that is local to the area, this can be a great place to stop for a little bit. Or, many tourists love to go here because they can see some of the real culture of the children and these make great gifts to take home for yourself or for others that you know. The paintings usually cost about $4 with the frame and you are helping support the arts and the children from Cambodia.

Banteay Srei

This is one of the temples that is the least visited in Siem Reap but this can be a benefit for you if you would like to avoid all the crowds and want to really see what all goes on in these temples. It is located way out on the outskirts of the other temples so it does take some time to arrive, but if you bypass the area and just go straight to this particular temple, you will find that it is really easy to have the place to yourself.

When visiting this temple, you should bring along a tour guide from the area. They will be the best at describing all the monuments and important parts of the temple as well as other information that you won't be able to find in the guidebooks, so you will have more fun and learn more on your trip. Try taking pictures a bit later in the afternoon because they will look so much better compared to some of the ones that you take at other times of day. If you are in the area of Siem Reap, this is really a place that you should stop and visit.

Preah Khan

This is another temple that is a bit off the beaten path, but this means more time for you to explore and learn and less time having to fight with the crowds. This is the perfect place to go if you are interested in seeing some of the old Khmer ruins, back before Cambodia was plunged into the dark ages that they are still trying to get out from. The area is beautiful and despite all the pillaging and wars that went on throughout the years, this temple has been able to hold on to some of its old glory.

Take some time to really explore this area. Most tours aren't going to even come and see this area, so make sure to pick one that does or schedule out some time to do it on your own. You are going to love all the little pathways and other fun things that you can do at this temple, and you will find that you can spend a whole afternoon just at this one place.

As you can see, there are a ton of great places to visit and things to see when you are in Cambodia. If you are planning on a vacation in this area, you are going to be able to choose from a wide range of events that are a lot of fun and can keep you busy the whole time that you are there. Make sure to book any tours ahead of time and fill out an itinerary that will keep you busy the whole time. In addition, take the time to try out a few activities that are a bit new or a bit out of your comfort zone. These are going to help you to have a really great experience while you are in Cambodia and it is easier to have an experience of a lifetime if you do something that can only be found in Cambodia.

CONCLUSION

Visiting Cambodia can be a great experience that takes you to a new world. There are a ton of great places that you are able to see and the people there are ready to greet you with warm arms. But it is important to understand the history that comes with this country and why it is sometimes difficult to get through the country or to see some of the great things that are in other countries. But with this travel guide, you will find that traveling to Cambodia can be a great experience and you are going to have a lot of fun!

WHY YOU NEED TO TRAIN IN THAILAND

Muay Thai Training, MMA Training, Wrestling Training, Thailand Travel Guide

Brandon BK Kesler

Copyright 2015 - All Rights Reserved – *Brandon BK Kesler*

ALL RIGHTS RESERVED. No part of this publication may be reproduced or transmitted in any form whatsoever, electronic, or mechanical, including photocopying, recording, or by any informational storage or retrieval system without express written, dated and signed permission from the author.

INTRODUCTION

Why train martial arts in Thailand? There are many places to train in Muay Thai, MMA, or Martial Arts, so why Thailand. You could go to Brazil and train in Jiu jitsu, or go to Holland and train in their world famous Kickboxing, and while both would be wonderful places to go and train, let me tell you why I, and many others, decided on Thailand to be the centre for our training. The answer is mathematical in nature; once I knew I wanted to train and fight full time I began considering a number of different countries. I was getting older and it was now or never as far as I could tell. Last thing I wanted was to be was seventy-years-old, sitting on my rocking chair and thinking to myself "man, I wish I would of done more." That's just not me; I have always been a man of action. My research considered the things most important to me: Quality of training, cost of living, quality of life, and the safety of the country.

I started out really leaning towards Brazil: beautiful beaches filled with sexy girls and their big fat asses, wearing nothing but G-strings, and, oh yeah, they have pretty good Jiu jitsu there as well. However, the expense of Brazil was more than most people would anticipate, and I had only a small amount of savings to my name. I started thinking maybe this was not the best choice, even though I could just not get the thought of those G-strings... I mean Jiu Jitsu Schools, out of my head. So I went to my best Brazilian friend Carlos, and asked him how safe it is to live and travel in Brazil. Carlos answered bluntly and said, "at some point you will definitely be robbed." I asked if he meant, like, with a gun robbed. Carlos said "yes, like robbed with a gun or knife, your just too white for Brazil." Well shit! Brazil was out for now; I had no intention to get held-up at gunpoint.

I researched Holland and other countries in Europe; they passed the safety criteria but were well over my budget. I'm a small town lower-middle-class guy from Washington. North and South America were out, so was Europe. So I started thinking South East Asia might be a better option.

The Philippines managed to meet everything I was looking for, but it didn't feel right; I don't know if I had just seen the movie Kickboxer too many times, but the idea of training in Thailand was filling my mind. Everyone I asked and everything I looked at said Thailand was cheap as hell with tons of gyms to choose from, and let me tell you, they were right!

Thailand has gym options for days: Muay Thai Gyms, Boxing Gym, MMA Gyms, Jiu jitsu Gyms, Judo Gyms, Fitness Gyms and more. When it comes to safety everyone will tell you Thailand is extremely safe. I have been living here for about two years and never had a real problem, or at least one that I didn't help instigate. This book will go much further into the cost and quality of living in Thailand for trainers, but let's just say you get a big bang for your buck!

In this book I will explain exactly why I train in Thailand and why you should too. If you want to be a professional fighter or you already are, but are tired of the bullshit that comes with living in the stress filled environment of your home country then read on and I will show you the beauty of living and training in wonderful Thailand.

STRESS FREE LIFE SAY BYE TO THE BULLSHIT

It's 5pm and you have been slaving away at your job since 6am, when you are just about ready to go home your boss comes to you and asks " hey do you think you could work a few hours overtime we are really behind." You tell him you have a fight in two weeks and you have training at 6pm. Your boss just looks at you funny, as if to say "a fight really", like he doesn't remember you telling him you had a big fight coming up.

This is the kind of thing that puts you at a disadvantage to the full time fighter who does not have to have a full-time suit-and-tie job, the fighter that just spends his days training two or three times a day.

Quite possibly the best part about Thailand is getting rid of all the stress and bullshit that can really drain a fighter when he is preparing for competition. While training in Thailand I only have to worry about one thing: my next fight. Life here is so easy to deal with that I don't even have to think about it.

Training in my hometown of Washington State typically went like this: Monday to Thursday I wake up and do thirty minutes of cardio on my elliptical before work, then I'd do an eight or nine hour day before going to train at the local gym with room full of amateur fighters and hey, I love them all, but they're all doing the same as me, working all day then showing up to training drained, putting in one and half to two hours of training when they can. By the time Friday rolls around nobody shows up for training and at the weekends the gym is usually closed. Once or twice a week I will drive to Victory Athletics located in Tacoma Washington, about an hour and thirty minutes from my home. The training is great but three hours of drive time sucks! Not to mention I know guys who are traveling three hours each way to train there. Yes I know there are other gyms in your city that are open for training all day, but not in every city, and not in mine.

Now let me tell you how the typical training week goes in Thailand. I'm a bit older and I put in about twelve or thirteen sessions a week, but the smaller and younger guys are doing up to sixteen sessions a week. I wake up about 7:30 am and go straight to team training for an hour and a half where we will do hard sparring twice a week and normal training technique the other four days a week. After that we have a quick breakfast then it's off to Cardio or lifting for about an hour, then the day is all yours to chill out and relax so you can get your energy back for evening training which alternates between wrestling, Brazilian Jiu jitsu, Boxing and Muay Thai. Keep in mind that all these classes are taught by high level coaches: all black belts or Pro fighters with many years of experience. Everyone is on the same page so they push each other to reach their goals.

The choice is always yours as to what kind of training you want to do. If you have a Muay Thai fight coming up then you can obviously skip the BJJ class and just attend the Muay Thai classes, or vice-versa, if you need to work on your wrestling then you can attend the classes that you and your coaches think are best for you. Most of the real MMA gyms in Thailand are filled with classes teaching all styles of combat all day long. It's very nice to choose your own schedule and work on the training style that fits your needs.

LIKEMINDED PEOPLE

Steel sharpens steel! If you want to be rich then find the wealthiest people you can and become friends with them. If you want to be smart then find the smartest people you can, and if you want to be a good fighter then find the best coaches and the best fighters and become best buddies. This is why when you were growing up your parents they did not want you hanging out with the little shitheads around the corner: shitheads breed shitheads. You are a product of your environment so pick your friends, training partners, coaches, and even girlfriends wisely.

Training in Thailand is excellent for this because you will find a large number of friends and fighters that are all working towards the same goals. If you are willing to work hard and help them, they will do the same for you. I always say if you're not getting tapped or beat up at your gym then you're at the wrong gym. You need to be at a gym that pushes you to your limit and forces you to work on your weaknesses while building your strengths. If you are overly comfortable at training this could result in a negative outcome, think about it, you're not going to be comfortable in a fight. When you are fighting in front of a large crowd, possibly with cameras broadcasting on television, how nervous do you think you will be? How much anxiety do you think you will have? If you are not used to this kind of pressure then this could be a real problem.

Now let's take into consideration you have been kicking the shit out of all your training partners for the last three months. This can be good because your confidence should be through the roof. However, how are you going to feel and react when your opponent is not as easy to finish as your weak training partners? If you're not used to overcoming adversity who knows how you will respond?

This is it is important to find likeminded people as well as good training partners. You should have a good variety of training partners: some guys you can easily dominate and try new moves on, a number that are right at your level, and some **guys that** really put it on you.

White Belts

The guys that are way below you skill level are great for many things. The guys who are either smaller, weaker, have less technic, or who are just not as athletic as you are great to use as practice dummies. You can try new moves, give up bad positions and work from there. You can also sharpen your best moves and even try stuff you never would when sparing with someone close to your skill level. This makes it very easy to go outside your comfort zone and to be creative and think outside the box.

Fighting at Your Level

Partners who are right at your level are possibly the best kind of partners to train with. This is debatable, but I think when you have two guys who are close in talent they are constantly going back and forth in winning and losing. Equal fighters make each other get better so they can keep up, this can often create some crazy athletes. You will often see this in brothers of similar age; take for example the Diaz brothers Nick and Nate, both are extremely skilled, and both have a very similar style. I would be willing to bet these two have been training back and forth for years. Finding training partners who are very close to your level of fighting, as well as similar in weight and body type, can be very advantageous in improving your skills.

Killers

You need to be losing in order to be learning! If you don't have a number of guys at your gym kicking your ass from time to time, then like I said before, you're at the wrong gym. This does not mean you have to leave your current gym high and dry, it just means you need to think, about your options. Your current gym should understand you need to train elsewhere, at least part-time, when you have no one pushing you. If not then they are not thinking of your best interests and that says a lot right there.

When you have training partners that are at a higher level then you are you will discover what really works and what doesn't. There are a lot of bullshit moves out there that will work on beginners and white belts but fewer moves and techniques that work on high level athletes. When you work with the top guys you will learn this very fast.

After Team Training Team Quest Thailand

MUAY THAI SPORTS CAPITAL

In the USA we have baseball, in Mexico they have Soccer, and in Thailand they have Muay Thai. Muay Thai is the National sport of Thailand and everyone has done it, from eight-year-old girls, to retired taxi drivers. At most gyms the trainers will have around two hundred fights under the belt, yes, you heard me right, two hundred fighters or more is not uncommon. I just recently meet an eleven-year-old Thai boy at Thai Phae Boxing Stadium with fifty four fights, that's fucking crazy! He is eleven-years-old and he has double the amount of fights I have. Impressive to say the least, but you have to remember that most of these kids start fighting at about the age of ten and they are fighting two to four times a month, possibly more, only to then retire in their mid-twenties. Many of these Thai fighters and trainers have a crazy amount of knowledge and experience that is unmatched anywhere else in the world. Where else other than Thailand could you find someone with this kind of real fighting experience? In the States you would be paying big dollars to get coaching or private lessons from athletes of this caliber, but in Thailand it is readily available for mere dollars.

Private Lessons

Think of this, if I was to get a private lesson from say a good Muay Thai training in the States this would cost be between twenty five and sixty dollars a session, maybe more. However in Thailand you can have a professional fighter with tons of experience gives you a private lesion, between one hundred and fifty baht to five hundred baht depending on the city your training in. As of 2015 that is between four dollars to thirteen dollars, and I would say at most gyms it will be well under ten dollars for private sessions. I personally know fighters who pay around two dollars for trainer to hold pads for five rounds. So once you get to know the guy and make some friends the price can even get cheaper! In the states or your home country you typically have another fighter or regular member of the gym to hold pads for you and these guys are typically quite inexperienced pad holders. If you're lucky the coach might hold pads a few rounds, but it would be impossible for one coach to hold pads for all the students. In Thailand most gyms have a large amount of Trainers and pad holders so there is no problem finding someone to train you.

The Clinch

Coming from a wrestling background I thought I had a pretty good clinch as we often train the fifty-fifty over under hook position. But what I did not realize when I first came to Thailand was that the Muay Thai clinch is so different. It was blowing my mind how this hundred and fifteen pound guy was sweeping me and controlling me in the clinch. I also did not realize that Muay Thai has a number of different sweeps and throws, it's not all kicks and elbows.

Knees

Once you have been kneed in the gut by a real Muay Thai fighter then you will know the importance of knees. These guys have crazy knees that are fast and come when you least expect them. Give them a bit of room in the clinch and that's the end of it. No matter how big and strong you are a hard knee to the liver when you don't expect it will drop you. Learning these techniques from guys who have been throwing knees since they were five years old is another huge advantage to training in Thailand.

Elbows

Mastering the elbow techniques is huge and even more important would be learning the defense to these nasty weapons. All it takes is one well-placed elbow to open a cut on your opponent and the fight is over! If you are not used to striking with elbows or you have not trained with fighters who attack with elbows on a regular basis, then you are at a big disadvantage when you start competing. Some of the elbow technics you will learn in Thailand are very sneaky and can really surprise someone. This is also a great way for the weaker competitor to inflict a large amount of damage without using much energy.

Micheal, Saenchai, BK and Juke in Bangkok

MMA GROWING FAST

When I first arrived to Thailand back in 2010 there was only one Professional MMA promotion in Thailand called "DARE Fight Sports" among several that were big in the rest of SE Asia. Now there are multiple promotions in Thailand alone and tons throughout SE Asia, as well as East Asia. The MMA community and MMA promotions are on the rises like never before. UFC PPV events are now shown on basic Thai television, while you are paying a ridiculous sixty dollars to watch PPV back in the States, we are watching it for free on basic Thai TV! Some of the Local Thai amateur MMA events are hosting over 60 fights in one night. Before there were only a few MMA gyms and they were located mostly in Phuket, now you have MMA gyms in cities all across Thailand, from Phuket to Chiang Mai.

Full Metal Dojo is one of the big players in Thailand MMA and it is offering fights almost on a monthly base. These are small to medium size shows but they are shows that will get you a lot of recognition in Asia, and even in the States, as they do an excellent job with promotions and media exposure.

Ching Mai Fighting Champion Ships, Thailand Ring Wars, and Bangarag Fighting Championship are smaller shows that mostly cater to fighters in the North of Thailand but will occasionally contract fighters from Bangkok as well.

Ole Baguio Laursen is also having shows in Ubon at Legacy. Tiger Muay Thai holds monthly amateur shows and there are big amateur shows in Bangkok on a near daily basis, as well as some large grappling tournaments that are mostly hosted by the guys at Bangkok Fight Lab.

There have also been some very large promotions stopping by Bangkok including Abu Dhabi Warriors and Kulun Fight. These are large promotions with pretty good payouts.

So if you're looking to compete there is no shortage of MMA events to keep you busy, just get out there on social media and start making some friends.

BEAUTIFUL WEATHER AND SCENERY

B E A U T I F U L! If you like hot sunny days and beautiful weather then you are sure to love Thailand. From the beautiful Islands of the south to the clean air and gorgeous mountains of the north, Thailand is a beautiful place to live and train alike.

I am getting a bit older and have had many gym wars as well as wars in the cage, not to mention the streets, so to say my body has some wear and tear is an understatement. When I travel home to Washington the first then I notice is how stiff my body feels. It takes twice as long to warm up and I never really feel as loose as I do when training in the heat of Thailand. Yes the heat takes a few months to get used to, but it is so much better on your body, and the result is far fewer injuries. Think about it like this, when you stretch a rubber band in the freezing cold, how likely is it to break or tear compared to when your stretch it in the heat of the sun? Our bodies work in the same way. I promise you this, your flexibility will improve and the amount of pulled muscles and injuries you get will have will drastically reduce while training in Thailand.

There is just something about waking up to the beautiful sunny days that always seems to put a smile on my face. I love training in this kind of weather and it seems to motivate you to go out and get your train on. Much different than when I'm training in cold countries and I don't even want to leave the house.

Thailand is a bit like summer vacation but it lasts all the time: jumping on your bicycle and cruising around your neighborhood, the kids are out playing, everyone is outside with smiles on their faces and the atmosphere is relaxed and chill. In Thailand that's how I feel everyday when riding my scooter around, it's almost like time travel. You have to experience it to understand it, but once you have you will fully understand.

LEVERAGING YOUR MONEY

The ability to leverage your money in Thailand sits at the top of the list of things that makes Thailand so great for training. When I first came to Thailand I had a few thousand dollars and I made this stretch out for a year and a half of living. Thailand is one of the cheapest places in the world to live considering the quality of life you get for the money you pay. You could sell a $5,000 car, buy a one way ticket to Thailand, and then live here for six months on that alone, you just need half a brain and some budgeting sense. I spend around $800 a month and I live like a king.

COST OF LIVING

Here I will give if a basic breakdown of living cost for me in Thailand.

- $120.00 Rent for a one bedroom studio right next to the Team Quest Thailand gym that I train at
- $10.00 to rent a flat screen TV
- $5.00 a month to rent a large fridge
- $5.00 a month for bedding (I could buy this but washing is included in the price)
- $3.00 for internet
- $5.00 for Cable TV with a few English channels
- $30.00 for water and electric
- $10.00 a month on fuel
- $20.00 to have my laundry washed and folded
- $10.00 a month to have my house cleaned
- $60.00 a month for protein supplements and vitamins
- $300 a month for food (I spend about $10.00 a day but meals are only about $1 to $1.50 for a basic Thai-style meal or around $5.00-$7.00 for something extra special)

If my math is right this comes out to about $578.00, though I spend another $100-$200 on random shit. So let's just say I spend $800.00 a month, but I know guys who spend $300 -$400 a month, some even less.

Everything is cheap in Thailand so I never have to think too hard about whether I can afford something, however if I'm traveling in Europe or the States that is a different story.

To compare the costs of living, seeing a movie in the USA costs $13 while watching the same film in Thailand could cost you only $5. A massage in the States costs about $70 per hour versus a massage in Thailand at $5. Eating out at nice restaurant in the states might cost from $100 to $150 but eating out at a similarly nice restaurant ranges between $20 and $80 in Thailand.

Obviously there are some places in Bangkok that are very expensive, but when you are comparing apples to apples the price is drastically lower. Let me give you an example: when I was visiting Stockholm I had a dinner with my girl at a normal burger place downtown. It was a nice place but nothing over the top, just you basic country-style burger joint. My girl and I both had cheeseburgers and shared a bottle of house wine, but the cost for this very normal, very average dinner? One hundred and thirty five US dollars.

Days before going to Sweden I had the chance to take my girl to a very beautiful rooftop bar located forty floors up with a spectacular view overlooking the whole of Bangkok. We both had delicious steaks, mixed drinks, and we split two bottles of a nice red wine, and the cost for this lovely night out? Ninety five dollars and that was with the most expensive steaks on the menu.

So yes, you definitely get a big bang for your buck when comes to Thailand!

HOUSING CHOICES

I spend roughly $800 a month to live and just under $200 of that is going towards my housing. I chose this house because it was the best deal on a property that was right next to the gym I wanted to train at. However, you can get a really nice studio or one bedroom apartment for about the same price and it will only a ten minute drive to any gym in Chiang Mai. Phuket and Bangkok are a bit more expensive, but, again, it really just depends where you live in those cities and the type of accommodation. When I was living in Bangkok I had a nice studio only a few blocks from the gym I was training at for $200 a month and I know friends who have houses for just a bit more in Phuket. I would say Phuket is the most expensive city in Thailand, followed by Bangkok and Chiang Mai is the cheapest of the big cities. All the cities have advantages and disadvantages so where you go depends on what you're looking for.

My house while I was training at Gym Bangarang *in Mae Rim Thailand.* **Cost: $ 252.54 a month**

CITIES TO LIVE IN

There are a large number of cities you can stay while training in Thailand and nearly every city in Thailand will have multiple Muay Thai gyms. However if you are interested in MMA gyms then they will mostly be found in the bigger cities. In this section I will go over the most popular cities for foreigners to train in while living in Thailand.

BANGKOK

Bangkok the capital of Thailand and my first love! Bangkok definitely has the best nightlife if you're into the party scene; BKK has clubs and nightlife for days. Considering Bangkok has about eleven million people, or more, it can be a bit crowded and getting around can be a headache at times. But if you bear this then Bangkok has much to offer if you want the big city life at a fraction of the cost. It is a poor man's New York City if you will. BKK has everything including rooftop sky bars, massage parlors, strip clubs, high end restaurants, Go Go bars, shopping malls, and night markets; you name it and Bangkok probably has it. As far as MMA gym goes I would only recommend one GYM in Bangkok, the Bangkok Fight Lab, they have great a new facility with world class trainers and a large number of training partners.

PHUKET

Phuket was probably the first area to bring MMA to Thailand with the famous Tiger Muay Thai. Phuket is filled with tons of traveling tourist as well beautiful beaches and numerous islands to explore. There's a nice party scene in Phuket if you're looking to get out when you have free time or when you're celebrating a win. The main reason I have avoided living in Phuket is the cost of living, it is double the cost of Chiang Mai, but the beaches are tempting. Someday in the future I will have to give it a shot. Phuket has a large number of Muay Thai gyms, but the biggest MMA gyms would have to be Tiger Muay Thai, Phuket Top Team, and the AKA Thailand. I have only trained at PTT for a couple weeks and enjoyed its facilities, but I'm sure all these gym have great things to offer.

CHIANG MAI

Chiang Mai has become my city of choice. I love Chiang Mai for several reasons. I think it has the best weather and cleanest air being owing to its higher elevation. One of the problems with living in Thailand is being hassled by the local Thai sales people or Tuk-Tuk drivers when you walk down the streets of Bangkok or Phuket, but you don't get this in Chiang Mai. You feel more like a local which is a breath of fresh air. The cost of living is the cheapest of all the big cities but there is still plenty to do. Team Quest Thailand is located in Chiang Mai and I truly love their training style because it truly fits my style of fighting.

Chiang Mai offers so many things to do that it has become one of the biggest destinations to visit in Thailand. Chiang Mai has people from all over the world either living here or just passing through, including Europe, Asia, and the States. You can choose from a variety of activities including rock climbing, bungee jumping, hiking, zoos, night markets, restaurants, and bars; between all of this you will have no problem finding something fun to occupy your free time. Not to mention everything is priced very well.

The downside of Chiang Mai is that there is no beach and I have yet to find a good Korean spa for after training recovery. But I love spending my rest days at one of the local pools located at one of many nice hotels. You can get a day pass to use these pools for around three dollars US.

Phil, BK, and Chris at local Bar in Chiang Mai

PATTAYA

I do not recommend Pattaya. As far as I, or anyone I speak to, can tell the city is simply for sex tourism, yes, they have some MMA and Muay Thai gyms, even some MMA promotions there, but it is truly a sin city. If you want to take a weekend with the boys then by all means have some fun but this is not a place to live long term. Too many distractions and too much filth, this is just my opinion but I would rank Pattaya last on my list big cities to train in.

THAILAND FOOD

About a dollar fifty!

That's what I pay for most of my meals. The food is absolutely delicious and extremely affordable. I literally eat out one hundred percent of the time. Yes, that's right, I don't cook! I ether go to one of the local Thai restaurants and have some delicious Thai food, or I just order from the restaurant at my apartment and have in brought to me. Yes, room service is still only about one dollar and fifty cents US!

If Thai food is not your thing then no problem, you can still get western food at a great price. When I was living and coaching MMA at 13 Coins Gym in Bangkok Thailand I would often have a double filet mignon for about five dollars, try and beat that back in the States!

Not only can you get normal Thai and Western food, but many of the restaurants near the big camps in Phuket and in Chiang Mai have health food restaurants nearby which are still a great price. Here in Chiang Mai I will often have an all organic meal with an all natural strawberry shake for just four dollars. Freaking Delicious!

FREE TIME ACTIVITIES

There are so many great things to do with your free time in Thailand depending on where you live. From surfing on the islands to hiking in the hills of the north there is no shortage of cool stuff to see and do. In Chiang Mai we have bungee jumping, paintball games, elephant camps, zoos, The Tiger

Kingdom, hundreds of restaurants and bars, fitness gym and Cross Fit gyms and more.

CHEAP SHOPPING

Prada or Gucci copies for everyone!

Thailand is known for its counterfeit and knockoff goods and just about everyone is walking down the street with fake Oakley with an armful of other fake gear, but hey, we all look good. I like to say get in where you fit in and have some fun spending five dollars on cool looking designer shades or some authentically fake Nike shoes. Remember everything in Thailand in negotiable, never pay the first price you are offered in Thailand.

"Forgiveness is divine, but never pay full price for late pizza" - TMNT

Not only can you get fake versions of everything at low prices, but the boxing and fight gear that is sold here comes at a great price! No need to pay the crazy prices back home; you can get your muay thai shorts, boxing gloves, sauna suits, or whatever you need and at a reasonable good quality. I guarantee you will be saving some cash when outfitting yourself in Thailand.

Not: MMA gloves are available in Thailand but they are not as popular, and puffers (MMA sparing gloves) are nearly impossible to find.

MASSAGES FOR ABOUT FIVE DOLLARS

When you are training every day up to two or three times a day then a massage or trip to the sauna is perfect for recovery. When living in the states you would go broke getting two or three massages a week; however this is commonplace in Thailand and is one of the big perks of training here.

One of the worst parts of returning home to the States is I cannot get a massage. Once you have become used to the unrivaled Thai massages found all over Thailand then the shit they call a massage back in your home country pales in comparison, and here the price is just a fraction of what it would in the USA or Europe. Shit, it's a fraction of a fraction. Back home I pay seventy to eighty dollars for a mediocre massage, but the average price in Thailand is only five to seven dollars, *how can you beat that?*

Just to be clear, I am talking about the normal massages, they do have the other kind as well, which run around fifteen US dollars, so if that's what you're into then Thailand is the place for you!

BEACHES AND BEAUTIFUL VIEWS

When you're not training or you have a day off from training it's nice to be able to just relax by the pool or beach, or to just check out some great scenery. Whether you decide to do your training in beautiful Phuket, my home of Chiang Mai, or even Bangkok, you won't have a hard time finding some great places to chill out. Thailand is full of water parks, rivers, beaches, pools, and just about anything you could want to swim in.

PEOPLE FROM ALL AROUND THE WORLD

When you only train in your city or local area you all end up learning and recycling the same techniques, tips and tricks. However, when you travel abroad you meet wonderful people from all over the world and what always amazes me if the fantastic new things I can learn. Just the other day I was telling a guy from the UK about my book, "IF You're Not Cheating You're Not trying" on how to cheat in combat sports. He says to me, "yeah I like to put hairspray on my feet when I fight on a vinyl canvas." Fucking genius. That is just one example, I'm always learning to techniques and tips from fighters from different countries. I am a big believer in cross training and when you are training in Thailand it's like you're always cross training, because you're always getting new groups of guys from all over the world to spar with.

It's like a melting pot of information and fight techniques!

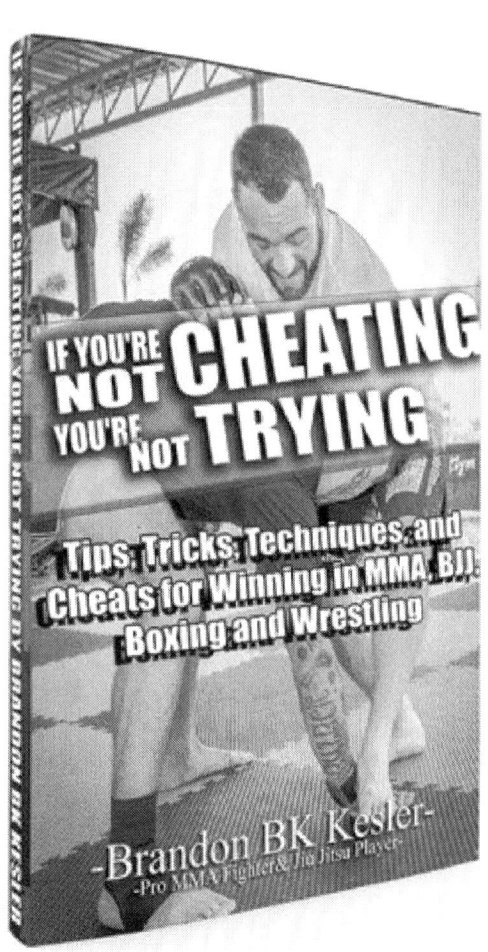

Outdoor Training

I am from Washington State where it rains oh, I don't know, pretty much always. It is cold, it is gray, and it is wet. Ninety percent of the time we have what I would consider bad weather. I train at a number of gyms back home, and don't get me wrong, I love them all, but there is a nothing better than training outdoors in heat of Thailand.

When I return home to visit my family, even if I return in the summer, the first thing I notice is my joints start hurting, I walk more stiffly, and it takes twice as long just to warm up. In Thailand I never pull a muscle or get hurt due to an improper warm up.

To be fair, the heat can take a while to get acclimatized to, but I believe it gives you a big advantage. When you are training in the heat every day you burn more calories and work much harder than when you train in a temperate climate.

The beautiful weather and atmosphere will also motivate you. It's true. I get excited to leave my house every day when I am training next to palm trees and scenic views. Compare this to the gym in your home where you most likely look out to grey skies, traffic jams and dumpsters.

Working my Muay Thai at Gym Bangarag

DON'T BRING SAND TO THE BEACH

Thailand has some of the most beautiful people in the world, either living here or just stopping by on holiday. Thailand is what you would call a melting pot, it has for travelers from all over the world so there are a large variety of people from everywhere, which means, most importantly, that there is a large variety of beautiful women from just about every country in the world, and who doesn't like beautiful women?

THAI GIRLS

Thai girls are probably the most beautiful type of Asian women, I'm sure it's debatable and really it's just a preference, but I think everyone will agree that Thai ladies are at the top of any list. Not only are these women very beautiful but they are also very nice and typically like to talk, flirt, and have relationships with foreign men. In many other Asian countries you would have a hard time getting with some of the women, but in Thailand they welcome you. The ladies of Thailand are very caring and will do just about anything for you. Think back to the 50s and 60s in the States where the women knew their place. Ha ha, just kidding, but you get my point, the women of Thailand are rather old school in many ways and this can be a nice change of pace.

With the all the dating websites and apps you would half to be a complete fucktard if you could not hook up with a beautiful Thai girl in Thailand. You have a huge advantage if you are a westerner and particularly if you are a white male, as white skin is thought to represent high class in Thailand. It's funny a quirk of Thai life as you will see many pretty Thai girls walking down the street with an umbrella out on a ninety degree day trying to hide from the sun to keep their skin from getting darker.

This also leaves darker skinned Thai girls easily available as they are thought to be lower class; it is not uncommon to see a white male who is at best a five or six dating a Thai girl who would easily be considered a ten in your home country.

Songkran Thailand's New Year's

FOREIGN GIRLS

To be perfectly honest I'm not really into Asian chicks, but luckily for me Thailand has some beautiful women from all countries living here. Many of the girls are going to college, teaching English, studying massage or Yoga, and these girls all have something in common, they are all beautiful. Well most of them. I have met girls from Sweden, Australia, Switzerland, Africa, Holland, UK, America, Germany, and India, just to name a few. You will literally see ladies from everywhere. As I write this book I'm currently in a relationship with a beautiful girl from Sweden who I never would have met had I not decided to move to Thailand.

Take some chances, you never know where life will take you!

HOW TO GET TO THAILAND

Moving to Thailand is a big step. You will need to get many things in order to make the big move.

First and foremost you will need some starter cash, I would recommend around five thousand dollars or so depending how long you are planning to stay, but many guys move here with much less and end up staying a long time. The amount you need depends on you.

Decide if you want to just sell everything, put anything you want to keep in storage, or find a friend or family member to look after some of your thing. I recommend selling as much a possible since if you do decide to stay in Thailand for a long time your things might become obsolete or worn. No need to hold on to a PS4 when they will probably have a PS5 by the time you return. If at all possible, I would find a close friend to watch your things or store your stuff in a friend's garage or shed. Storing with friends is free, and when living in Thailand we really want to have as little responsibility as possible, that way we can focus on our training.

If you own your car you could easily sell it to finance your trip and live on those profits for a year or more depending on how much its worth. If you have a lease you will need to plan your trip accordingly, or talk with whoever owns the loan and see about getting out of your lease early. In Thailand a five hundred dollar scooter will do the trick just fine, or you can rent one for about forty dollars a month.

If you rent you will need to see when your lease is up or talk with your landlord about getting out of your lease early. If you own your house you could do what I did and give your property to a property management, or have one of your close friends or family members live in it and collect a small fee from them. Most property management only charge around eight percent of the rent you make, but be careful, I had given my property to a management company that was nickel and diming me to death, so letting my family take care of the property was the better choice for me.

Once all the big stuff like your house and car are taken care of, you could have a large garage or estate sale, or sell them on a listing site like Craigslist; this is how I financed my first trip to Thailand. I simply placed a few ads in the newspaper, craigslist, and on a few social media pages and waited for the buyers to roll in. I left everything in my house exactly where it was except for a few tables filled with smaller things and had a large estate sale. I made almost $4,000 selling my bed, TV, pool table, stereo, PS3, old records, pots and pans, clothing, and just about everything I could. It's crazy how much crap we acquire over the years that we really don't use. Replacing old things when and if you decide to return is easy with Craigslist and Facebook groups. When I returned home for the first time I got everything I had before only they were new and upgraded. If there is one thing were good at in America it is buying shit.

So look around your house, find the stuff you can live without and do some price checking to see how much you think you can come up with. You might be surprised!

PASSPORT AND VISA

First thing's first if you don't have a Passport then apply for one. This normally takes about four to six weeks to get. If you need it in a hurry you can do an express application, I had to do this when I booked a trip to Mexico and had to change destinations to Fiji, because at that time I did not have a Passport and my vacation was only two weeks away. Luckily there are several states where you can go in person and apply for a rushed Visa, which normally only takes two days to get. This was a few years back and things could of changed so please don't quote me on this, you may need to do a little research first. But one thing is for sure, you're going to need a passport.

Once you have received your passport you will need a Thai visa. If you're coming from the States you will get a thirty day visa on arrival without any prior application, so If you plan on staying longer I would suggest getting a double or triple entry visa to start with. This will give you two month, with a one month extension, so about ninety days in total. Then you will have to make a short trip to Laos or Cambodia so you can cross the border and come back and get another ninety days. If you get a triple entry you can do this just twice then you can stay for nine months without any issues.

When your double entry is getting close to expiring you have the choice of either going to Laos, getting another double or triple entry, or you can apply for a student visa to learn the Thai language. These visas will give you one year in the country without you having to leave; you will simply have to check in at Immigration every ninety days. Really this is the **best** option and is the visa I'm currently on. Not only is it the most cost effective visa and avoids you having to make numerous border runs, but you get to learn Thai at a very affordable rate.

For a one year visa I paid only **12,500 Baht** which comes out to **$355.746** plus about **$56.00** every three months to renew, so you're looking at about **$579.79** for the whole year, which comes out to **$68** a month for visa and School. Not Horrible for a year visa and a year of Thai language lessons.

Now I know half of you are thinking, cool, I would love to learn Thai, and the other half of you are thinking I don't have time for that shit I need to train. Well good news, most schools don't really care if you attend class, in fact the one I'm at now really does not care and has never mentioned any non-attendance. However if you don't want to go to class that is fine, but I do suggest learning some Thai as it will help you experience living here in Thailand better.

I learned the majority of my Thai language skills on YouTube, [Pimsleur Thai on my iPod](), and one-on-one lessons which I paid around five dollars per two hour session for.

Note: visas are always changing for Thailand so do your research before you come.

CHEAP TICKET

Typically when I'm booking my tickets I have found that by booking about forty five days in advance you can find the cheapest tickets possible. I will check at least three sites: Skyscanner, Orbitz, and Expedia. I will normally only book my ticket to Bangkok online as I can connect by myself at a fraction of the price to other cities by just booking my connecting flight to the smaller provinces right at the airport. If say I was at Don Muang the international airport and booked a ticket to Chiang Mai on the same day I would normally pay about forty five dollars, Phuket will be double or even triple that, but it is still inexpensive.

When booking your ticket make sure to always double check the luggage amount as sometimes you will be charged if your bags are too heavy.

GYM SPONSORSHIP

Ok, you're already a stud fighter and have a bit of name and real skills. This is good because gyms in Thailand love good foreign fighters and will sometimes offer partial, even full sponsorship to high level fighters. Tiger Muay Thai actually holds tryouts where the winners will receive one year of free sponsorship and Team Quest Thailand is always looking for promising young talent. I have been given a free week of training at Phuket Top Team a few years back just to go on Holiday there, and AKA Thailand will offer some sort of similar scholarship.

Depending on which gym picks you up, you could be giving free housing, training, even food or more. Make sure you really understand the details so there are no surprises for you.

You of course will have to represent your gym and wear their clothing and take their banners to all of your fights, you will also need to help them on social media, and represent their gym whenever competing. You might even have to give up a percentage of your winnings if they are the ones finding your fights and working as management for you.

Ok, now it's time to get sponsored. I suggest making a fighter profile page. This is the same kind of page you send to promoters and fight managers when trying to get fights. It's very simple to do, you will simply make a word doc or you can even just make it in a message from your email account.

Write a small bio about yourself, nothing too long. I wrestled in high school, have an amateur record of 5-2, I train at Brick house Gym with UFC fighter Jimmy Jones, I'm a pink belt in Kesler Karate, etc. You get the idea.

Then find your best pictures, about four or so is enough, and send two pictures that are post type pictures in a "standard fight pose" and two action type pictures. Make sure you send these in high definition as they might use one of these to go on their website, or for promotion on social media down the road. If you don't have any good pics everyone and their mom has a good camera or something decent on their phone. Find a friend and take some fight pics next to white wall. Make sure you're wearing fight shorts and not jeans.

Next upload your highlight real.

Shit, you don't have a highlight real? Don't worry these days it's very easy to make one for only about twenty dollars. If you think really hard you probably know a friend that can help you and there is software just about everywhere for editing, but I do suggest having a professional do it for you to beat out the competition. Look on Fiverr.com and I'm sure you can find someone for twenty dollars or less. If you're a broke ass bitch and don't have twenty dollars, well, you probably can't afford to come to Thailand anyway. But you could just upload some of your good fights and that will probably do the trick.

HOW TO MAKE MONEY IN THAILAND

Ok great, well you have either sold all your old crap, gotten a sponsorship, saved up money from your shitty nine to five job, taken your pay from your last fight, won the local dance contest, or whatever, but now you have a pocket full of cash and are ready to make the move to Thailand. But wait, that money won't last forever, and you will need to make some cash while you're in Thailand. There is a number of ways to make cash in Thailand: fight Muay Thai, fight MMA, fight K1, fight boxing, teaching English, acting or modeling, becoming a digital nomad, or opening your own business.

I have some friends that will literally fight two, even four times a month. When I first met UFC vet Will Chope, who at that time was not UFC, he said he started fighting like crazy, doing MMA, Muay Thai, and K1 in just about every country in South East Asia and East Asia. He went from having a few fights, to over fifty fights, including fighting in the UFC in only about two years or so after started fighting seriously. So if you're looking for a place to get fights there is no shortage in Asia.

BK fighting in China

FIGHTING MUAY THAI

Muay Thai fights are readily available; you could literally fight three times a week if your body would allow it. I have friends fight three, even four times a month. However these fights do not pay very much, not much at all to be honest. For most fighters who are twenty fights and under, we are talking around fifty dollars to three hundred dollars a fight. Then when you get very big the payouts are still much lower than in boxing, MMA, and K1.

But if Muay Thai is your love or you just want the experience, shit, maybe you just like have having your thighs kicked to shit, I don't know. Either way, you can most definitely make a few bucks fighting in Thailand, but don't have any false hopes of becoming rich, because the best Muay Thai fighters in the world still don't have very much money compared to other combat sports athletes.

<u>Bangarang Fighting Championships</u>, **Mae Rim Thailand**

BOXING

Boxing is not nearly as big in Thailand, but there are shows and the pay is much more than Muay Thai. When I first came here to Thailand I was training at 13 Coins and I met a Thai trainer by the name of Juke. He was a retired Muay Thai Champion turned boxer. He was training for a boxing match and getting about a thousand dollars per match. The owner of the gym let me and another foreigner travel with him to watch the fight. Juke won by KO in the second round. Only a few months later Juke was competing for the WBCA title and getting a few thousand dollars a match. He had no one to train him; he was teaching Muay Thai and training himself after work. I felt rather bad for him and would hold pads for him after my training every day up until the fight. When the fight finally came around the owner of the gym asked me to corner him, but I said only if there was a Thai corner as well, because at I could not speak Thai for shit then. Juke ended up winning a hard fought decision against a tough Filipino fighter.

I ended up leaving Thailand about a year later and Juke kept fighting, when I returned after two years of living in the States. I stopped by my old gym and asked how Juke was doing. The owner told me he was a fighter on the undercard of Manny Pacquiao and getting about fifty thousand dollars. This is serious money to a Thai guy. He ended up losing the fight but he got paid, so fuck it, that's still a huge come up.

I also have taken a boxing match, not in Thailand, but in China for pretty decent money. The great thing about Thailand is if you're a tough fighter and make a little noise you will get offers from all over Asia.

So if boxing is your thing or you're a MMA fighter with a good hand and just want to make some cash on the side then boxing is another option to get paid.

After the fight interview

FIGHTING K1

So like I mentioned before, there is a lot of opportunity to fight, not only in Thailand, but elsewhere and the real money is in surrounding countries, particularly in East Asia. Just recently I started taking some K1 fights in China, I figured I could use the extra cash and there only three rounds and three minutes to a round, much better than the five, three minute rounds of Muay Thai. The pay for beginner K1 varies but if you're a decent fighter getting one - three thousand dollars for a fight is not uncommon. But most fights are around the fifteen hundred dollar range and when you're living in Thailand on a budget of around 750 dollars a month this will finance you for about two months. Think how many Muay Thai fights at fifty bucks a pop you would have to do to earn that much money.

Risk Versus Reward.

Chinese promoters or fight managers will fly you from Thailand to China and back with a corner man. Some fight managers will ask you to stay and take multiple fights depending on your durability; this can be a good way to stack up some cash. I just recently fought twice in five days and came home with a nice payday.

K1 Fight in Shanghai China

FIGHTING MMA

MMA is growing like crazy in Asia, not to mention Thailand. Now the pay-per-view UFC is shown for free on TV and has Thai commentators giving you the breakdown. Yes, the very same events you pay sixty dollars for back in the states is shown at just about every home in Thailand for FREE. Of course there is a time difference here so instead of watching the fights at normal seven o'clock in the evening we get up early and watch them at about nine in the morning, but not a bad way to start your Sunday-Funday, AKA the rest of day.

With the growing popularity of MMA in Thailand we are seeing new promotions and events popping up everywhere and now is the perfect time to get on board. There is Full Metal Dojo, probably one of the best known events in Thailand that took the place of Dare, the old leader of Bangkok Thailand MMA. But now there aren't just events in Bangkok, we are also seeing events in all the smaller provinces like Chiang Mai, Phuket, Pattaya, and Udon. And even some of the large Muay Thai promotions like Abu Dhabi Warriors are adding MMA fights to their events. It is becoming more common to see mixed promotions filled with both Muay Thai and MMA fights and I believe we are going to see more and more as time goes on.

With all the new promotions and events being held throughout Thailand you can be sure that if you're a decent fighter you can definitely make some cash and get on some of these promotions. However, Thailand does not pay that great, but hey; the cost of living in Thailand is quite cheap. If you're looking to makes some good money there are tons of large promotions all over East Asia looking for good talent. These promotions love foreign fighter that are based in Thailand because it saves them money on airfare and they would much rather build up an Asia based fighter that can easily fight for them several times in a month, rather than a fighter based in the States or in Europe.

Some of the top promotions in Asia would have to be: One FC, Deep, Pancrase, Shooto, Top FC, Road FC, VTJ, IGF, Kunlun Fights, and FMD. Now if you have already made your fighter profile like I suggested before and you have decide to come to Thailand it might be a good idea to hit up your Facebook page and start liking some of these promotions. After you have arrived in Thailand and you think you're ready for a fight send out some messages asking these promotions if you could send them your fighter profile and tell them you are based in Thailand and would really like a fight on their show. Make sure you are ready to go, because if you do everything I said you will be surprised how many promotions will contact you, however, sometimes it is on short notice and you need to be ready to fight. There is nothing a promoter hates more than you asking for a fight then having you say, "oh well I was thinking in a few months or so," YOU ARE NOT IN THE FUCKING UFC! You don't always get a full ten week training camp. If this was perfect world maybe, but this is the real world so always be ready.

Dare Fight Sports in Bangkok

OTHER WAYS TO HUSTLE CASH

Ok, so maybe you're not quite a professional fighter, but you still want to train in Thailand and make some cash. There are a number of other ways the most common would be: teaching English, acting, modeling, digital nomad, business owner, or straight up hustling.

TEACHING ENGLISH

Teaching English is probably the most common Job for foreigners in Asia and especially in Thailand. There is large community of teaching English based in just about every major city. Getting a job at a public school should be quite easy especially if you have a college degree of any kind and English is your first language. However, I know a ton of guys with no degree whatsoever who teach English, some without even a high school degree. This obviously depends on what school you end up working for, but I'm sure a small public school paying around twelve hundred dollars a month will be much easier to work at, compared to a job at an international school paying three or four thousand a month.

I'm not a professional on this topic, as I'm a pro fighter not a teacher, but I meet loads of teachers here who are all making a decent living. I had a friend who was a pro Muay Thai fighter who had a pretty sweet deal working only two eight hour days on the weekends which left him the whole week to train. He was pulling in around a thousand dollars a month, more than enough to live in Thailand. Then all his money from fighting was play money. Not a bad set up.

If you want more info on this top I would suggest checking out some Teachers of Thailand Facebook groups and asking some questions. Facebook group

ACTING OR MODELING

Shit, but I can't act and I'm anything but a model. Well neither am I but guess what; I have done three commercials without even trying. The good thing about Thailand is there not that much competition when it comes to certain niches. For example I have a friend who probably is not the best actor in the world but always gets steady work because he is a big white guy with big muscles and how many big white guys with muscles are there in Thailand? And how many of those guys are trying out for acting or modeling gigs? Not that many. So when you show up to audition and there are only a few other guys, the chances of getting the gig are pretty good. Compare that to Hollywood where hundreds of guys show up to auditions.

I did a rugby commercial once. The audition took only about an hour, most of the time was spent waiting in the lobby with a room full of beautiful models from all over the world. At the time I was like holy shit, I'm just going to keep coming here just to hang out in the lobby, fuck the acting job. After a few days passed they notified me that I got the gig and told me where to show up. The job only took about four hours and I was paid three hundred dollars. Not bad at all.

These jobs can vary heavily from job to job, ranging from extras work at about fifty dollars a day, to large gigs for big companies paying upwards of five thousand dollars. Being fit and in shape, not to mention have a background in martial arts can definitely help. I have several friends who are always getting gigs in action movies.

If you would like to get some gigs I would suggest checking out these [Facebook groups](#)

Note: Bangkok would be best for acting and I would only suggest living here if I wanted to make a living as an actor or model in Thailand.

Rugby Commercial in Bangkok

DIGITAL NOMADS

Digital nomads, the art of working wherever you want from your own personal computer. Nowadays there are so many ways to make money online I would need to write another book on it. But one example would be this book. Because I don't work a nine to five and have quite a bit of down time it frees me up to write a number of books which can pull in some additional cash on a monthly basis. This is something that would be much more difficult living in the states where most people trade their most valuable resource "their time" for money.

Digital Nomads are just about everywhere in Thailand and in Asia, but it seems like the number one destination would be Chiang Mai. These guys are doing everything from drop shipping stores, affiliate marketing, selling goods on eBay and Amazon, writing eBooks, Blogging, Podcasts, and just about everything under the sun.

If you're good at something online, or like my Dad likes to say, *"On the line,"* then you can make money. You can either sell your service to someone else on a platform like Elance, Odesk, or Fiverr, or you could start up your own website, blog or affiliate store. If you consider yourself an expert on a topic then write a book about it.

I have made a bit of money selling my books here on kindle which really helps to finance my stay here in Thailand.

OPEN YOUR OWN BUSINESS

Many people come to Thailand and open their own business and many people go home singing the blues. This would be my last choice unless you have run businesses in the past and have a real knowledge of business and of Thailand. Owning your own business in Thailand can be very profitable due to the fact that many things are very cheap: rent, employees, food, etc. But there is also a lot of competition so unless you're thinking outside the box and, like I said, have some real experience, you're taking a big risk. At the same time fuck it, if your dream is to own a sunglass shop or restaurant in Thailand, then go for it, just be careful. One of the major problems with owning a business in Thailand is the fact you can legally only own forty nine percent of the business and the other five one has to be owned by a Thai national. What the fuck right?

Well I never said Thailand was perfect I only said it was a great place to live and train to fight. Many foreigners have opened businesses, usually with their Thai girlfriend or wife, only to end up with nothing more than a sad story.

There are ways to get around this and if you are considering opening a business I would suggest talking with an experienced lawyer. I have met a number of people in Thailand with successful business, everything from MMA gyms, fitness gyms, restaurants, hostels, scooter rental shops, and clothing stores. Owning a nice business in Thailand if definitely doable, just be careful, take your time, and double check everything.

DON'T BE A PUSSY! TAKE SOME ACTION!

This is the problem with most people. Everybody everywhere at some point in their life comes up with some great idea, maybe it's a cool invention, maybe it's dream to travel through Africa, maybe there is a beautiful girl you are secretly in love with; whatever this great idea or thought is, most of the time people think to themselves, oh shit, this is awesome, but then by the end of the day that dream is just that, nothing more than a dream. Maybe they told their friends or family members and they gave them back a list of reasons why this idea would not work. This is a big problem for most people in life as they listen to others who are also afraid to take risks, sometimes you have to just roll the dice and see where they fall.

"If you don't help yourself no one is going to help you."

Sometime after you share this great idea everyone you tell thinks the idea is absolutely wonderful, but then you yourself start to talk yourself out of it. You start coming up with lists of problems and obstacles in your head, and before you know it you have created a huge wall of doubt and a mountain of reasons why you should not carry out this wonderful idea. I know if you think hard enough you can come up with many reasons or problems not to do this great thing, but if you really try you can come up with a plan on how to beat those problems. As fighters we need to be strong mentally and physically.

No, I'm not saying you should jump into anything blind; I'm all about doing research and taking the right steps to achieve your goals and dreams. What I am saying is this, take some fucking action! Stop being a pussy and do the shit you want to do. I don't care if you want to be a fireman, produce a rap album, sail across the ocean, or make a million dollars. If that's your dream then take the necessary steps to get there. If you have always thought how fun it would be to travel the world, or train and fight in Thailand then book a ticket. The worst thing that will happen is you move back to right where you are now. I guarantee it.

Thank You!

Thank you so much for reading my book! I hope you have enjoyed it and learned a thing or two. It would mean a great deal to me if you would [please leave a review](#) for me as they really help the sales of books!

Made in the USA
San Bernardino, CA
02 July 2016